THE CIVIC WEB

Campaigning American Style

CAMPAIGNING AMERICAN STYLE

Series Editors
Daniel M. Shea, Allegheny College
F. Christopher Arterton, George Washington University

Few areas of American politics have changed as dramatically in recent times as the way in which we choose public officials. Students of politics and political communications are struggling to keep abreast of these developments—and the 2000 election only feeds the confusion and concern. *Campaigning American Style* is a new series of books devoted to both the theory and practice of American electoral politics. It offers high quality work on the conduct of new-style electioneering and how it is transforming our electoral system. Scholars, practitioners, and students of campaigns and elections need new resources to keep pace with the rapid rate of electoral change, and we are pleased to help provide them in this exciting series.

Titles in the Series

Campaign Mode: Strategic Vision in Congressional Elections
   by Michael John Burton and Daniel M. Shea

The Civic Web: Online Politics and Democratic Values,
   edited by David M. Anderson and Michael Cornfield

Forthcoming

High-Tech Grassroots: The Professionalization of Local Elections
   by J. Cherie Strachan

THE CIVIC WEB

Online Politics and Democratic Values

EDITED BY
DAVID M. ANDERSON
AND
MICHAEL CORNFIELD

ROWMAN & LITTLEFIELD PUBLISHERS, INC.
Lanham • Boulder • New York • Oxford

ROWMAN & LITTLEFIELD PUBLISHERS, INC.

Published in the United States of America
by Rowman & Littlefield Publishers, Inc.
A Member of the Rowman & Littlefield Publishing Group
4720 Boston Way, Lanham, Maryland 20706
www.rowmanlittlefield.com

PO Box 317, Oxford, OX2 9RU, United Kingdom

British Library Cataloguing in Publication Information Available

Library of Congress Cataloging-in-Publication Data

The civic web : online politics and democratic values / edited by David M.
Anderson and Michael Cornfield.
    p.   cm.—(Campaigning American style)
Includes bibliographical references and index.
ISBN 0-7425-0193-0 (cloth : alk. paper)—ISBN 0-7425-0194-9 (paper :
alk. paper)
    1. Political participation—United States—Computer network resources.
2. Political campaigns—United States—Computer network resources.
3. Internet—Political aspects—United States.   I. Anderson, David M., 1958–
II. Cornfield, Michael, 1955–   III. Series.
JK1764 .C52665   2003
320.973'0285'4678—dc21   2002000281

Printed in the United States of America

♾ ™ The paper used in this publication meets the minimum requirements of
American National Standard for Information Sciences—Permanence of Paper for
Printed Library Materials, ANSI/NISO Z39.48-1992.

CONTENTS

Part III   Citizen Participation and the Internet

Part IV   The Internet, Democracy, and the Future

FOREWORD

F. CHRISTOPHER ARTERTON

OVER THE LAST DECADE, political organizations have increasingly turned to online communications to conduct many of their major activities. Through e-mail and web pages, they perform such essential tasks as contacting voters, recruiting activists, fundraising, reaching journalists, communicating within their organizations, and mobilizing voters on election day. Although this trend is in its infancy (no one can seriously claim that online communications are yet a major component of campaign strategy), the direction is certainly upward.

There are growing signs that democratic politics will increasingly be conducted online in the decades to come. Most journalists, organized interest groups, political action committees, trade associations, corporations, political parties, and individual activists are using sites on the World Wide Web so that audiences of citizens and activists who bother to take the initiative can ascertain their goals, messages, and policy objectives. The image of the Web as a massive library has certainly propelled many of the politically active to use its vast resources for policy and political research. And political organizations of all stripes are also building e-mail lists, creating listservs, and producing online newsletters that allow them to reach an expanding roster of online citizens.

At the same time, over on the receiving end of political communications, an increasing roster of Americans—college students and senior citizens, wealthy people and those of modest means, men and women—are using the Web to glean information relevant to politics. In 1996, only 4 percent of the public went online to retrieve news about the campaign. This increased to 7 percent by 1998 and 16 percent in 2000. Among Internet users, 31 percent in 1996 reported that the Net helped them in making a decision for whom to vote, a percentage which rose to 36 percent in 1998 and 40 percent in 2000. Moreover, since the number of Internet users in 2000 was five times as large as in 1996, the rise is greater than these percentage increases suggest.

The available data indicate that the online media are penetrating American society at a rate only slightly slower than television. By the spring of 2001, 59 percent of Americans had Internet access at home (167,744,287 in April 2001 or 59.06 percent).[1] Penetration of households tends to be a bit more concentrated; a year earlier 41.5 percent of U.S. households had access to the Internet (i.e., 43.6 million households in August of 2000).[2] A comparable level of penetration (42 percent) of U.S. households by telephones was achieved in 1928, and again in 1943,[3] after recovery from the Depression and World War II. Radio penetration reached 42 percent of U.S. households in 1930[4] (12,040,000 households with a radio set out of 29,905,000).[5] Television achieved this level by 1953.[6]

While the data are imprecise, the information presented in the table provides a comparative assessment of approximately how long it has taken different communications media to reach half of the households in the United States. By this measure, the growth of the Internet seems to be proceeding at a fairly rapid pace. Of course, there can be a wide gap between the public's access to a medium and its use as an effective means of political communication and civic learning. *The Civic Web* is less about the demographics of the medium and more about the evolution of a useful tool for expanding democracy.

As Michael Cornfield has written, "The growth period will not last forever. When it concludes, patterns of online behavior in public life will largely be set for a generation. Furthermore, the distinction between 'online' and 'offline' media will have vanished, thanks to the convergence of multimedia forms on what will become broadband infrastructure maintained by a concentrated industry. Citizens will go to this enhanced Net as a matter of habit, to see political messages they may have heard about on the radio, or glimpsed on a billboard, or, more likely, seen in paid advertising embedded in entertainment programming. The transition between incoming advocacy and self-initiated inquiry will be relatively seamless. Citizens who wish to learn

Communications Media Penetration in U.S. Households

Technology/Medium	Years To Reach 50% Penetration
Newspapers	100+
Telephone	70
Phonograph	55
Cable TV	39
Personal Computer	16*
Color TV	15
VCR	10
Radio	9
Black & White TV	8

Sources: Electronic Industry Association; U.S. Dept of Commerce, and www.ksg.harvard.edu/iip/doeconf/carey.html.
*To reach 40 percent penetration.

which candidates are running for political offices, what they stand for, and who is supporting them will expect to find the answers online."[7]

We think democracy requires that those answers be timely, substantive, and from a variety of perspectives. This is the fundamental mission of the Democracy Online Project from which this volume has emerged. In three years of operation, the Democracy Online Project (DOP, or Project) has come to be regarded as an authoritative voice on the topic of online politics. The project's mission encompasses research, publication, education, debate, and advocacy addressed to a range of audiences including candidates and their campaigners, political party committees, advocacy groups, civic organizations, election officials, journalists, and citizens. We aspire to encourage practices in which this new tool of communications will underwrite, rather than undercut, the values of democratic politics. We offer this volume, *The Civic Web*, as a contribution to this important debate.

Among the forces that influence the development of communications media, one must include technological invention, financial investment, social needs, and cultural values. Although we cannot yet predict how online politics will evolve, the Democracy Online Project is dedicated to nurturing a debate over the values of democracy, a debate that can make an important contribution to this evolution. As a society, we will be better off if we consider how we would like this medium to evolve *before* it happens than we will be if we wait until the medium has achieved its formative growth and then try to recast it. The authors included in this volume have directed their arguments and comments to that end.

Notes

1. www.nielsen-netratings.com/ The United States actually crossed the 60 percent threshold of access to the Internet in January 2001 according to Nielsen-NetRatings. However, the numbers declined somewhat in the following months. See www.newsfactor.com/perl/story/7497.html.

2. NTIA Report on Americans' Access to Technology Tools, at search.ntia .doc.gov/pdf/fttn00.pdf.

3. Report on the Deployment of Advanced Telecommunications Capability to All Americans, CC Docket No. 98-146, FCC 99-5.

4. Historical Statistics of the U.S.—Colonial Times to 1970, U.S. Department of Commerce, Bureau of the Census, Vol. II, Kraus International Publications 1975, 796.

5. 20th Century Statistics, U.S. Census Bureau (Statistical Abstract of the United States: 1999, 873).

6. Report on the Deployment of Advanced Telecommunications Capability to All Americans, CC Docket No. 98-146, FCC 99-5. Also visit: www.tvb.org/ tvfacts/tvbasics/basics1.html.

7. Michael Cornfield, *Politics Moves Online*, forthcoming.

ACKNOWLEDGMENTS

I N PUTTING TOGETHER this collection of essays, we received advice, assistance, and encouragement from a number of people. Sean Treglia of The Pew Charitable Trusts was crucial to the funding of the Democracy Online Project, which brought us together and inspired this book. F. Christopher Arterton, Principal Investigator of the Democracy Online Project and Dean of the George Washington University's Graduate School of Political Management, has encouraged us throughout.

Our thanks go to Ronda Brown, the Associate Director of the Democracy Online Project, and to six different research assistants who helped us at different stages of the process: Ryan Thornburg, Akis Skertsos, Juraj Droba, Don Baker, Nicholas Stark, and Julie King. To Julie King we owe a special debt for her significant help in editing all of the chapters. We are also grateful to our editor, Jennifer Knerr, for her support, guidance, and patience.

Finally, some personal thanks. Anderson wishes to express his thanks to his wife, Adrienne, and his stepson, Simon, for their love and support. Cornfield wishes to thank his wife, Kathy, for love, inspiration, and their new son, Matthew.

INTRODUCTION

Michael Cornfield and David M. Anderson

I N THE LAST DECADE of the twentieth century, something new
and exciting—the Internet—was introduced into something old
and treasured—democracy. Although electronic mail and other
forms of information exchange among a dispersed network of computers had been in limited use for more than twenty years, the advent
of the World Wide Web and the Web browser in the 1990s rapidly
expanded the presence of the Internet in American life. Entrepreneurs
attached the "e-" prefix everywhere, including the public square—the
place where politicians, citizens, and mediators speak and act on the
issues of the day in forms and forums open to all. The campaign web
site was, in 1996, a novelty. In 2000, it was a news trend. By 2004, it
will be a political staple.

Of course, no one can know whether the Internet is going to have
a major impact on democracy in the United States. To some, the
Internet is precisely the technology our tired democracy needs and
will ultimately be used for the better; to others, the Internet is just
another communications technology that will become absorbed into
our ongoing institutions without altering the distribution of power or
the level of political participation by citizens. And then there are many
people who have yet to really think about the question at all.

This collection of original essays should prove useful to anyone
with a sense of curiosity about the possibilities that exist with the
Internet. The authors of the chapters come from different stations in
our society, and they represent different ideological viewpoints. Some
of the authors are academics, some work in policy institutes, some are
from activist organizations, and two are from a law firm. The chapters
themselves reflect a range of writing styles. Some are grounded more

1

in empirical research, some are more conceptual in nature, and some draw heavily on specific experiences in the online politics community. We think the new and sprawling topic of online politics and democratic values suits the variations in style you will encounter in this book.

The Civic Web: Online Politics and Democratic Values embodies our hope that online politics will develop in harmony with democratic values. Freedom of expression, citizen participation, social tolerance, government accountability, and public deliberation are among the ideals we associate with such a "civic web." The contributors to this volume show that this hope is not unrealistic. Networked communications can host, and even advance, enlightened self-government by a free people under the rule of law. This book will show, however, that a civic web will not be easy to realize.

Part I of *The Civic Web* raises a set of fundamental issues about ways the Internet might be used to improve our democratic institutions. The opening chapter, by Deborah G. Johnson, identifies three characteristics that set the Internet apart from other forms of human communication and elucidates the ethical implications of these three features for political campaigning. The Net is unique, first, because it "facilitates many-to-many communication on a global scale," second, because it allows individuals to disguise their identities, and third, because it greatly enhances the capacity to copy and alter messages. Johnson shows that each of these distinguishing qualities can help and hurt democratic politics. Much will depend, she concludes, on how society shapes the Internet for civic use.

David M. Anderson tries to remove a number of misconceptions about online politics in order to create a sense of "cautious optimism" concerning our ability to harness the Internet to improve our democracy. He argues that it is too soon to be cynical about the role played by commercial political web sites; he also explains how arguments that draw an analogy between the Internet and television (which did not fundamentally change citizen knowledge and action) are problematic. Anderson goes on to suggest that the area of politics that is most likely to engage citizens is issue politics, not election politics. By showing how people have a tendency to equate politics with elections and the Internet with an oversimplified view of "information," he helps pave the way for a more balanced appreciation of the multitude of ways that the Internet could be used to engage citizens in political action.

William Galston addresses one of the main threats the Internet poses to American democracy: increasing political and social fragmentation. He worries that the Internet may tighten the already disturbing hold that special interest groups wield in our democracy. The Internet makes it easier for people to find like-minded individuals and to communicate with them to the exclusion (deliberate or accidental) of other citizens who have different perspectives and priorities. That can inflame intolerance; it also places an awful burden on governmental and other institutions charged with integrating competing interests into common action. Galston backs a proposal to require the most popular web sites to carry links to a deliberately diverse array of public voices.

Election campaigns take center stage in Part II of *The Civic Web*. Peter Levine evaluates campaign web sites in the narrow, electoral sense of the word *campaign*. But the purpose of his assessment is anything but parochial. Levine looks at whether such sites adequately serve the general public interest by providing three civic goods: specific issue statements by candidates, maximum participation by voters, and an enlightening exchange of views by all (a.k.a. deliberation). He also considers whether "even if the Internet does not force campaigns to provide public goods, it might at least save them money." Levine concludes that these desirable developments will not flow from the campaigners' efforts alone. Rather, philanthropic individuals and foundations must create Internet sites that, together with legal reforms, can change the incentive structure in which campaigners operate.

The current state of election law as it pertains to the Internet is the subject taken up by Trevor Potter and Kirk L. Jowers. Although a hands-off approach has prevailed among most Internet regulators to date, the better to promote both robust discourse and business growth, the Federal Election Commission (FEC) has been a partial exception. The FEC has seen fit to constrain online campaign communication in which "the expenditure of large sums of money for overtly partisan political speech" is manifest. The agency has discovered, however, what a tricky matter it is to affix a dollar value to links and page views. Potter and Jowers review the relevant legislation and advisory opinions, summarizing what citizens, corporations, unions, candidates, parties, interest groups, and other political actors must keep track of as they campaign online.

Jerry Berman and Deirdre Mulligan illustrate four ways in which political actors have learned to use the Internet to influence public opinion and public policy. Their observations flow out of their experiences with the Center for Democracy and Technology, a Washington, D.C.-based advocacy group that has used the Internet itself to influence legislation about the Internet. The first and simplest means of online advocacy relies on e-mail to spread a message like a virus, by "word of mouse" if you will. Second, the Net has made it feasible for individuals and organizations to coalesce around a single action item instead of just a common cause. Third, the Net endows advocates with "the credible threat that they will make some uncomfortable fact public;" advocates can go public without having to convince the media that their information is news. Fourth, advocates can facilitate communication from citizens to governments and businesses. The Internet, in short, greatly enhances the advocates' arsenal.

That said, it is by no means clear that the Internet simplifies advocacy for the average citizen. Part III looks at the civic web in terms of the general populace. As Michael Cornfield illustrates by recounting his own efforts to reduce airplane noise in his neighborhood, getting one's voice heard can be a bewildering odyssey even with the advantages the Internet confers. He distinguishes between "keyword intelligence," issue information that the Internet supplies in abundance, and "password intelligence," strategic information that rarely surfaces online. Both types of information are required for political success. The Internet lists strategists for hire, but enlisting a professional advocate in one's cause is no easy matter unless one has a lot of money. Then there is the challenge of staying engaged and motivated as a campaign wends its way through the public square. Cornfield suggests one feature that could help sustain involvement: online "civic participation counters" that keep running totals of the progress a campaign is making.

Anthony G. Wilhelm praises government and private initiatives that seek to close the digital divide, but he cautions that universal Internet access alone will not create digital citizens. Much more is needed to engage citizens in the democratic process than providing them with computer hardware, software, and Internet access. "Having an Internet connection does not lead ineluctably to the navigation of the civic web any more than owning a car leads a citizen to the polling station on election day." Wilhelm calls for programmatic boosts to "lifelong learning," a neo-Madisonian combination of formal and informal education opportunities. The civic web can engage the entire population with the help of schools, community centers, workforce development programs, mentors, and media support.

Michael X. Delli Carpini and Scott Keeter report that Americans know about as much about politics today as they did fifty years ago, notwithstanding great changes in the information environment (e.g., more sound bite journalism, less commitment to civic engagement). Even with that record of stability in mind, the Internet and other digital technologies may lead to profound alterations in the distribution and nature of political knowledge. The highly motivated may learn, and act on what they learn, as never before. The less motivated may find more ways to avoid politics. The unconnected may fall further behind. Specialized and generalized knowledge may go together, instead of the former advancing at the expense of the latter (as Galston argues in part I).

Part IV of *The Civic Web* offers three very different visions of online democracy. Steven Clift's spirited programmatic statement flows out of his experiences with Minnesota E-Democracy, an online public commons that he helped establish in 1994. (His chapter, more than any other in this book, treats the topic of "e-government.") Clift observes that for governments to be democratic, they must do more than just automate their delivery of services and responses to constituent inquiries; they must also disclose information and hold online public hearings. Drawing on examples from around the world, Clift substantiates his belief that "over the next few decades we can change democracy for the better and develop 'wired' ways that enable people to improve their lives and the world around them."

Langdon Winner is not so sure. His historical review shows that, in the United States, dreams of democratic renewal have often accompanied new transportation and communication technologies into public life. It was no coincidence that both the Erie Canal (1825) and the Baltimore and Ohio Railroad (1828) were opened on Independence Day. However much these dreams resound in society, Winner warns, they cannot be realized without transformation of political and economic institutions. He wonders aloud whether today's Americans will demand anything more from the Internet than "more bandwidth, more sports, more movies, and a wider range of opportunities for shopping." If they do not, then corporate appeals to consumers will dominate the Internet, as they did in the "new media" that preceded it.

Michael Vlahos invites us to imagine a "network world," a quantum leap beyond the "world with a network" we currently inhabit. As accessing the Internet becomes second nature, people will identify less and less with the geographic jurisdictions into which political power is now divided and more and more with "communities of affinity," groups of people with similar interests and outlooks who may live anywhere on Earth. The nexus between civic life, on the one hand, and the city and nation-state, on the other, will dissolve. "A person's primary affinity group will eventually be recognized as that person's primary civic—and thus, political—affinity as well." People will seek justice, representation, and governance in a radically altered context. This will be a change in human consciousness commensurate with the fall of Rome and rise of Christianity. American values, including democratic values, may well triumph, but the supremacy of American government may give way to new arrangements between individuals and worldwide organizations.

Although any book about politics and democratic values is always somewhat dated by the time it reaches publication, books about Internet politics and democratic values run the risk of being more dated than usual. The Internet speeds everything up. Still, the chapters in this volume were written with the longer view in mind. We are confident that even as some of the political web sites authors discuss have vanished, new political web sites will appear in their places during the next election cycle or when a particular issue generates the need for new organizational structures. Thus, the vagaries of public life on Internet time notwithstanding, we believe the authors have limned the essential issues, opportunities, and dilemmas posed by the meeting of computer-networked communications and democratic politics in the United States. We hope their concepts and arguments will help you understand, and find your place in, the digitized public square.

THE INTERNET AND POLITICS: FRAMING THE ISSUES

Reflections on Campaign Politics, the Internet, and Ethics   1

DEBORAH G. JOHNSON

IN BOTH THE POPULAR PRESS and scholarly literature, the Internet is often depicted as a democratic technology, or at least as having the capacity to enhance democracy and democratic institutions. Although claims about the connection between the Internet and democracy are complex, multifaceted, and contentious, political campaigning is seen as one aspect of democracy that could be significantly enhanced by the Internet.

To understand how the Internet has already affected political campaigning and is likely to affect it in the future, it is helpful to begin with what is new and unusual about the Internet. In what follows, I describe three features of the Internet that distinguish it from other forms of communication, and I draw out the implications of these features for political campaigning. The three special features are many-to-many global scope, the availability of a certain kind of anonymity, and the property of reproducibility. I have identified these three features in other writings with particular emphasis on their ethical significance;[1] here, I will draw out their implications for ethical issues in campaign politics.

The major ethical issues in political campaigning have generally been understood to be fairness of competition and quality of information. Do the "rules of the game" and the actual activities of campaigns create conditions of fair competition? Is information circulated during the campaign accurate and candid or deceptive and manipulative? In short, does the campaign process have integrity? This chapter examines the special features of the Internet with an eye toward the democratic character and integrity of political campaigns. The question of the chapter is this: As the Internet becomes more and more a part of political campaigning, how are its special features likely to impact the democratic character and integrity of political campaigns?

Many-to-Many Global Scope

Comparing the Internet with face-to-face communication and with telephone, television, and radio communication suggests that the Internet is unusual because it has a many-to-many global scope. Many-to-many global scope refers to the breadth of reach and interactive character of communication on the Internet; it means that many individuals can avail themselves of an expanded breadth of reach and can communicate with many other individuals almost anywhere in the world. In other words, the Internet increases the communicative power of individuals. It is important to keep in mind that access to the Internet is not universal and is not likely ever to be universal, but the Internet is currently available to millions of individuals across the world. Any one of these individuals can, in principle, communicate with any other individual who has access and can do so quickly, relatively inexpensively, conveniently (from one's home), and easily (with only simple finger movements).

Taken separately, each of these aspects of Internet communication is not new and is available in other forms of communication. Although face-to-face communication does not have global reach, it is easy, convenient and immediate. Telephone communication is also easy, convenient, and immediate, and it has the same global reach as the Internet. Television and radio communication also have immediacy and the capacity to reach vast numbers across the globe. Moreover, from the perspective of the communicator standing in front of a camera or speaking into a microphone, radio and television communication are relatively easy to use.

However, none of these forms of communication has the combination of these features in the way that the Internet does. Although face-to-face communication is easy, convenient, and instantaneous, one does not have the ability to reach vast numbers of individuals across the world. Telephone communication is immediate and easy and has global reach, but the number of individuals that can be reached simultaneously is limited, and there is more inconvenience in the sense that it requires all users to be on the phone at the same time (simultaneity). Moreover, for now at least, telephone communication is more expensive than the Internet for reaching large numbers of individuals. Although radio and television have global reach and ease of use, they are one-way forms of communication. Information goes from the radio or television station to thousands or millions of people, but communication does not flow back the other way, and, of course, radio and television are too expensive to be available to many.

What is special about the Internet, then, is that it embodies all of these elements. It has global reach, convenience, ease of use, and relative low cost together with availability to many. With the Internet, many can communicate with many others cheaply, easily, conveniently, immediately, and across the globe. The Internet facilitates many-to-many communication on a global scale.

It is this characterization of the Internet as a facilitator of many-to-many communication on a global scale that leads to the idea of the Internet as a democratic technology or a democracy-enhancing technology. The visual image of a web of connections between individuals, a network of communication lines going from every individual to every other individual, suggests the possibility of a democracy like that of the ancient Greek city-state, with frequent and intense interactions between citizens on a larger scale. With this image in mind, we imagine individuals getting together frequently online to discuss issues of governance. We might further imagine individuals communicating electronically with local, state, and national political representatives and accessing government services online, as well as citizens forming special interest associations or organizing political movements. These possibilities are, of course, relevant to political campaigning because candidates for public office want to activate voters. They want to get information to voters, find out what voters think, hear what voters say, identify special interest groups, organize events, and mobilize supporters.

Yet it is important to remember that the Internet facilitates old as well as new patterns of communication. It can facilitate one-to-one, one-to-many, one-to-few, or few-to-few communication as well as many-to-many. The Internet is malleable, and its potential for creating new patterns of communication will not be realized automatically by its mere availability. Recent research suggests that the many-to-many (interactive) capacity of the Internet is not being used extensively by government and political campaigners.[2] The Internet is, for the most part, being used to facilitate a pattern of communication that predated it, namely a one-to-many flow of information from candidates (or campaign organizations) to citizens and potential voters.

Thus, although the Internet creates the possibility for interactivity on a grand scale, this potential of the technology might not be utilized for campaign politics. On the one hand, it seems plausible to hypothesize that the newest features of a technology would be the slowest to be adopted and used. It takes time for users to understand and figure out how to tap the full potential of a new technology. Thus, perhaps it is just a matter of time before political campaigns take full advantage of the interactivity afforded by the Internet. On the other hand, political campaigners may be more interested in one-to-many communication, in using the Internet to distribute more information more quickly and with more convenience. Indeed, the central unit—be it a campaign headquarters, a political party, or a government agency—may be reluctant to encourage constituents to interact with one another because the outcome of such interaction is difficult to control. The Internet makes it possible to involve a larger number of people in agenda setting and decision making, but when more people are involved, power is diffused. Some gain influence; others lose influence. So, it is possible that political campaigns and campaigners will not want to take advantage of the interactive capacity of the Internet. They may be more interested in sending information and shaping citizens than in involving citizens in agenda setting and decision making.

As mentioned earlier, the standard ethical issues in political campaigns are fair competition and accuracy of information. When we ask how these issues might be impacted by use of the Internet, it is not the interactive character of the Internet that comes into focus, but rather access and scale. The increased power that the Internet gives to those engaged in political activity is undeniable. The Internet allows political campaigners to distribute an enormous amount of information quickly, cheaply, easily, and conveniently, and it allows for this information to be updated frequently. The Internet has been portrayed as an inexpensive tool with the potential to level the playing field in many competitive environments, including campaign politics. The Internet is often described as a resource that gives power to the less powerful. For example, Jesse Ventura's campaign for the governorship of Minnesota was seen as a case in which a newcomer with comparatively meager resources was able—with the aid of the Internet—to beat two mainstream candidates who were more entrenched and had greater resources.

Yet this depiction of the Internet is somewhat misleading, for the Internet can be used both to help newcomers and to help old-timers.

The Internet can give power to the less powerful, *and* it can increase the power of the already powerful. It all depends on who uses the Internet and how. Those with greater resources can invest more in the use of Internet tools; they can develop better web sites, pay for links, and pay for priority in search engines.

It is also misleading to describe the Internet as a tool that helps the less powerful become more powerful, because this depiction focuses on those who use the Internet to campaign and pushes out of sight the issue of who is reached by the Internet. When attention is shifted from campaigners to citizens, access is a much more troubling issue. As mentioned before, the Internet is not universally available. When it is used successfully to inform and involve citizens in politics, it informs and involves only a subset of citizens, largely those who are wealthy enough to afford computers and Internet access.

The breadth of reach of the Internet is also often seen as a democratizing element because it allows alliances and special interest groups to form independent of geographic location. The Internet reveals how geographic dispersion prevents like-minded individuals from joining forces and acting together. As a result of the Internet, like-minded individuals who separately were ineffective minorities can join forces and promote their interests collectively. A wide variety of special interest groups have formed online, and the Internet allows these groups to form across local, state, and national boundaries and yet to have · frequent and extensive interactions. In short, the Internet eliminates the need for geographic closeness in the formation of political groups.

This creates a dilemma for politics. On the one hand, it creates the possibility of new and more representative influences on democratic decision making. On the other hand, it threatens local and national geographic sovereignty, for it means that individuals who do not live in a particular geographic area can have a powerful influence on political campaigns and political decision making in that region. The Internet increases opportunities for wider participation in political processes, but wider participation sometimes means more involvement of voters who are living outside their home state or country, and other times means more involvement and influence by those who are nonvoters and noncitizens. The disadvantages of outsider influence on political campaigns have been a theme in campaign financing.

So, although the many-to-many global scope of the Internet has the potential to impact campaign politics, its potential may not be realized. The many-to-many scope of the Internet will not of its own accord lead to more interactive political campaigns, nor may it of its own accord lead to fairer and more informative campaigns. Use of the Internet may instead exacerbate issues of access and outsider influence.

Anonymity

A second special feature of the Internet is its capacity for a certain kind of anonymity. Anonymity is a complex concept, and it would be misleading to say that people have anonymity on the Internet, as activities on the Internet can be monitored and traced. For example, most people with Internet access use an Internet service provider (ISP) at home or work, and these service providers keep records of people's activities. It would be more accurate to say that many of the signs of identity that we humans use in face-to-face communication (and in telephone communication) are not available on the Internet. In face-to-face communication, we identify individuals by seeing what they look like, asking to look at their driver's licenses, listening to their voices, and watching their behavior, and often we correlate these features with our memories of past experiences with the person. Though it depends on the particular technology being used (and the technology is changing), individuals who communicate on the Internet are anonymous in the sense that these signs of identity are not available: we can't see each other, hear voices, or examine driver's licenses. The absence of these signs of identity also means that individuals communicating on the Internet can be pseudonymous. Individuals can use multiple on-screen names and can take on different personas from one communication to the next. Of course, anonymity and pseudonymity are possible in face-to-face communication; individuals can disguise themselves by wearing masks and distorting their voices or simply by telling lies about who they are and what they want. Nevertheless, the inaccessibility of an individual's physical appearance (including his or her physical location) when communicating on the Internet is important to note.

Anonymity and pseudonymity have advantages and disadvantages for democracy and for campaign politics: The availability of anonymity and pseudonymity on the Internet seems to free individuals to engage in behavior that they might not otherwise engage in. For example, in contexts in which race, gender, or physical appearance may get in the way of fair treatment, anonymity may serve as an equalizer. Anonymity may also promote participation in beneficial activities such as discussion forums for rape victims, battered wives, or ex-convicts. Without the shroud of anonymity, individuals might be reluctant to participate in such forums because of the risk involved in having this aspect of their lives revealed. However, although anonymity facilitates participation in these beneficial forums, in other contexts, anonymity can allow individuals to avoid accountability for their actions and can free individuals to commit crimes and engage in socially undesirable behavior.

These two sides of anonymity are well understood in the context of political campaigns, in that they have a parallel in the American system of voting. Our nation's system of voting is designed to ensure that citizens vote anonymously: how a citizen votes cannot be determined by others. This frees all citizens to vote as they see fit. At the same time, the system must identify all voters to ensure that they are qualified to vote. Hence, various mechanisms have been developed for registering qualified voters and identifying them as they enter the polls but disconnecting the fact that one votes from information about how one votes. In other words, our voting systems balance the value of anonymity with the importance of identity.

A similar balancing will have to be done when it comes to political activity on the Internet. Citizens should have some form of anonymity in political activities so that there are no repercussions for their political actions and expressions. At the same time, there is a need for identity in many contexts to ensure environments conducive to democratic activities. For example, participants in online chat rooms and bulletin boards can be disruptive. A single individual can have undue influence by participating as multiple personas. Individuals can misrepresent themselves as members of a group in order to gather information to be used against the group or to sabotage the group by introducing false or misleading information. Thus, for political campaigns to take advantage of the potential of the Internet, it will be necessary to figure out ways to achieve an effective balance between anonymity and identity. Political forums will be more effective if there is some degree of confidence of the identity of participants and, at the same time, there is some degree of privacy to encourage political expression.

Reproducibility

The third special feature of the Internet is reproducibility. Reproducibility means that electronic information, including actions and transactions, on the Internet can be (and are) recorded and reproduced. The most salient implication of this feature is its challenge to common conceptions of property. Electronic property—programs, data sets, software, computer graphics—can be reproduced without loss of value and in such a way that the copying is not evident to the owner. The difference between traditional forms of property and electronic property is illustrated via a comparison between theft of an automobile and theft of a data set. In the former case, the owner no longer has the automobile and can see that it is gone, but in the latter case, the owner continues to have the data set and sees no sign of the theft.

Of course, reproducibility is not a feature of only the Internet but rather of electronic media in general. Yet, the Internet exacerbates the problems arising from reproducibility of electronic media by making reproduction possible via remote access; that is, individuals can record and copy information while being thousands of miles from the source. And though our legal and moral notions of property have been tested many times over the centuries by new inventions, information technology has been formidable in its challenge. The appropriateness of new electronic inventions for patent or copyright protection continues to be tested in the courts.

The challenge to property rights is not a central issue when it comes to political campaigns, but reproducibility creates another problem that goes to the heart of political activity in a democracy. The reproducibility of the electronic medium means that everything done in electronic environments can be recorded and reproduced, and this exacerbates the tension mentioned in this chapter's previous section between the value of anonymity and the need for identity. The Internet facilitates a degree of surveillance that has not been possible before.

The Internet is peculiar in that, while it gives users a particular kind of anonymity and a strong sense of being anonymous, the reality is that actions and expressions on the Internet are more traceable and more enduring than in many other environments. In face-to-face discussion, words are spoken and then they are gone (unless, of course, someone makes the effort to do audio or video recording), but on Internet interactions, a record is automatically created and the words endure (unless someone does something, e.g., deletes the record). So, on the one hand, individuals may experience a sense of being anonymous because they can't be seen, and yet at the same time their behavior may be more easily traced than if they interacted in a face-to-face environment while wearing a disguise. Unless this aspect of the Internet is managed judiciously, it could have a dampening effect on political participation.

The reproducibility of the Internet also challenges the integrity of information. Because of reproducibility (together, again, with a certain kind of anonymity), individuals can capture the words of others and do a variety of things with them. B can capture the words of A and send them as if they were B's words. Or, A can capture the words of B, change them, and then send them as if they were B's words. Capturing aside, A can create words and send them as if they were B's words. When it comes to campaign politics, the potential for abuse is great. Admittedly, many of these abuses are possible without the Internet. The Internet simply makes it easier to do more quickly and on a broader scale. The speed with which these things can be done, together with the scale on which they can be done, means that damage, once done, may be difficult to undo. Perhaps the best example is that of a false rumor spread across the globe in less than twenty-four hours. Recovering from a false rumor on the Internet is no small feat. How do you reach all the people who have read the false rumor?

Many of the problems arising from reproducibility are likely to be addressed technologically. For example, cryptographers are developing schemas and tools to authenticate identities and maintain confidentiality while at the same time protecting privacy. These techniques may succeed in balancing the desirable aspects of anonymity with restricted traceability, that is, traceability, only with a warrant. These tools may have a significant impact on the degree to which the Internet's potential will be realized.

Conclusion

The three special features of communication on the Internet—many-to-many global scope, anonymity, and reproducibility—have great potential for democratization of politics in general and for campaign politics especially. Nevertheless, these three features raise a number of serious ethical issues for political campaigning. The many-to-many global scope creates an enormous potential for interactivity that arguably could emulate aspects of the old Greek city-state democracy on a larger scale. However, the Internet also facilitates old patterns of communication on a larger and more intense scale, and this enables information to flow from one to many in an attempt to shape and manipulate voters rather than allow more participation. The global scale of the Internet also raises a serious question about outsider influence on campaign politics, because it allows individuals outside geographic areas to participate, and exert influence, electronically. The Internet also makes a certain kind of anonymity possible, a kind of anonymity that can encourage socially beneficial activities but that also creates problems in accountability. Whether or not the Internet is effectively used for campaign politics will depend on achieving a balance of anonymity and identity that is conducive to democratic politics. The reproducibility of communication on the Internet challenges traditional notions of property and privacy. It makes possible an unprecedented degree of surveillance that could threaten democratic processes and the integrity of information on the Internet.

These threats may be addressed with new technologies, but they will not be addressed unless euphoric beliefs in the democratic potential of the Internet are exchanged for sober acceptance that the Internet is a malleable technology and is socially shaped. It can be shaped for more or for less democracy.

Notes

1. D. G. Johnson, *Computer Ethics* (Saddle River, N.J.: Prentice Hall, 2001) 3rd ed.; D. G. Johnson, "Ethics Online," *Communications of the ACM* 40, no. 1 (January 1997): 60–69.

2. M. Hale, J. Musso, and C. Weare, "Developing Digital Democracy: Evidence from Californian Municipal Web Pages," in *Digital Democracy Discourse and Decision Making in the Information Age*, ed. B. N. Hague and B. D. Loader (London: Routledge, 1999), 96–115; P. Nixon, and H. Johansson, "Transparency through Technology: The Internet and Political Parties," in *Digital Democracy Discourse*, ed. Hague and Loader, 135–53; A. G. Wilhelm, "Virtual Sounding Boards: How Deliberative Is Online Political Discussion?" in *Digital Democracy Discourse*, ed. Hague and Loader, 154–78.

Cautious Optimism about Online Politics and Citizenship

DAVID M. ANDERSON

THIS CHAPTER SEEKS to eliminate some misconceptions that might prevent people from using the political Internet to its fullest potential. Much of the discussion is conceptual, as the chapter tries to clarify what online politics is and can be, but part of the discussion is empirical, as it presents encouraging data about the role the Internet is playing in the lives of citizens. Throughout the chapter, an effort is made to show that cynical arguments about the democratizing potential of the Internet are problematic; in place of cynicism, I set forth a path of cautious optimism.

Navigating Your Way around Political Web Sites

Moving around the world of politics by car, airplane, ship, cab, and subway is complicated enough; moving around the online political world is even more complicated because you can pay a productive visit to three or four completely different kinds of political organizations in a matter of minutes. The speed of the online world can make it difficult to know where you are.

For all newcomers to the civic web, and even for some veterans (those who went to political sites as early as 1996 or 1998), it is useful to separate different kinds of political web sites, because without a clear sense of the different kinds of sites, it becomes difficult to evaluate a host of criticisms concerning online politics. Distinguishing the different kinds of sites does not in itself settle any moral debates, but it does facilitate critical understanding and create a shared vocabulary for discussion.

I want to briefly present a taxonomy for classifying what I regard as the four main kinds of political web sites.[1] The taxonomy is composed of two cross-cutting distinctions:

1. nonpartisan vs. partisan
2. nonprofit vs. for-profit

The two distinctions can be combined to create four possibilities:

a. nonpartisan/nonprofit political web sites (usually dot-orgs)
b. nonpartisan/for-profit political web sites (usually dot-coms)
c. partisan/nonprofit political web sites (usually dot-orgs)
d. partisan/for-profit political web sites (usually dot-coms)

These four possibilities, with some examples of sites that were prominent in the 2000 election cycle, are shown in table 2.1.

As the framework illustrates, there are both not-for-profit and for-profit versions of nonpartisan web sites; these sites are heavily focused on voter education. Thus, there are nonpartisan political dot-orgs (the not-for-profit sites) and nonpartisan political dot-coms (the for-profit sites). The same holds at the level of partisan sites: there are partisan political dot-orgs and partisan political dot-coms.

Note that federal election law prohibits corporations from having partisan political web sites, but it does not prohibit limited liability partnerships and sole proprietorships from having partisan web sites. The partisan political dot-coms that I refer to are not corporate sites.

Table 2.1

Nonpartisan/Nonprofit	*Nonpartisan/For-Profit*
Project Vote Smart	Vote.com
Benton/Debate America	Voter.com
Democracy Project	SpeakOut.com
FreedomChannel.com (a not-for-profit site even though it uses the ".com" url)	GrassRoots.com
California Voter Foundation	GoVote.com
Partisan/Nonprofit	*Partisan/For-Profit*
Candidate sites	Democrats.com
Incumbent dot-gov sites	
Some issue advocacy sites	

The Democrats.com site, to take one example, is a partisan political dot-com because it is a for-profit organization that promotes the ideas and ideals of democrats. These partisan political sites, it is also important to note, are not legally permitted to engage in express advocacy for a candidate. They can, however, engage in issue advocacy. Some partisan sites, then, are express advocacy sites (e.g., candidate sites that advocate for themselves), and some partisan sites are not express advocacy sites (although they can be partisan toward a party and, by implication, its candidates).[2]

It's Too Soon to Criticize Commercial Nonpartisan Sites

We can now briefly address a concern raised by many during the 2000 election cycle, namely that online politics, like the Net overall, is becoming overly commercialized. For citizens and social commentators who are already cynical about politics, the nonpartisan political dot-coms—companies like Vote.com, Grassroots.com, SpeakOut .com—add fuel to the fire. Some people balk at the idea of a company taking on the task of educating the public about elections and issues. Because some political dot-coms are seeking to promote voter deliberation, education, and even communication with government officials, the concern has been raised that we should not let profit-making organizations get involved in these democratic endeavors. In his contribution to this volume, Peter Levine discusses some of the main objections to the nonpartisan political dot-coms. These include the objection that for-profit organizations will cater to the interests of the most well-funded supporters of their organizations and, in the process, will marginalize less well-funded, probably more extreme, political positions.[3]

Cynicism about commercial political sites, while not groundless, is not justified. For one, the political dot-coms (I'll focus on the nonpartisan variety, as the partisan ones are few in number) are not receiving enough traffic to be doing much harm. They still are a very young breed. Second, the political dot-coms, especially those that seek to promote voter education and deliberation, have many of the same stated aims as nonpartisan political dot-orgs. Because they are explicitly nonpartisan sites, people need to give these sites (or future sites of this kind) the benefit of the doubt. Third, the nonpartisan political dot-coms have developed sites with many customizing interactive features that could engage the citizenry in more effective ways than do the nonpartisan political dot-orgs, which tend to provide information in more straightforward ways. Dot-com sites may possess the excitement that is needed to bring politically disengaged citizens to politics. Through them, citizens who have passionate commitments to particular values and issues may find that the Net creates channels for their passion.

But even if we welcome a diversity of political sites into the online political world, we must ensure that the dot-com sites do not force the dot-org sites out of existence, a fear expressed by many during the 2000 cycle. History to date actually suggests that the political dot-org sites are more stable than the political dot-com sites, which rely heavily on venture capital and advertising income.

We must also be vigilant about protecting citizen privacy.[4] The commercial political sites—like any commercial web sites—are inclined to sell sensitive voter information because they must make a profit to survive. And although political dot-org sites (especially candidate sites) were criticized for their poor privacy policies—or their lack of privacy policies altogether—in the 2000 cycle, the profit motive makes the political dot-com sites especially vulnerable to criticism. Still, it is an interesting question whether selling voter lists to make a profit is a more ethically questionable activity than selling (or even sharing) voter lists to win an election. At this early stage in the development of online politics, the political dot-coms should be watched carefully but any deep cynicism about them seems misplaced.

TV and the Net Are Not Analogous

A second cynical argument concerning the democratizing potential of the Internet concerns an analogy drawn between the Net and television. At its inception, television (like radio before it) was hailed as a new communication technology that would lead to better-informed, engaged voters, but it failed to live up to that democratizing potential. The question now is whether the Internet will have the same fate.[5]

Attempts to draw a comparison between the Internet and television are relying on one of the most common forms of analogical reasoning: Object A has properties 1, 2, 3, and 4. Object B has properties 1, 2 and 3. Therefore, Object B, because it is analogous to Object A, also has property 4. As analogical arguments are inductive (as opposed to deductive) arguments, their conclusions can never be necessarily true. Inductive arguments generate conclusions that are more or less probably true, depending on how much evidential support the premises provide for the conclusions.[6]

A standard discussion about the television/Internet analogy becomes an analogical argument with the following problem. Television has properties of being electronic, being capable of reaching a mass audience, being a one-way form of information and communications technology, and not leading to more politically engaged citizens. But the Internet does not actually have the same first three properties; instead, it has the three properties of being electronic, being capable of reaching a mass audience, and being a two-way form of information and communications technology. The third property of the Internet is different from the third property of television: television is a one-way information and communications technology, and the Internet is a two-way information and communications technology. Although television and the Internet both provide information to viewers, the Internet allows users to make purchases, communicate with others, organize events, and donate money. Television does not.

This two-way property of the Internet, moreover, is very relevant to the question about political engagement, because the very interactivity of the Internet is what has made many people think that it might lead to more political interactivity in our society. Thus, the inductive inference to the conclusion that the Internet "will not lead to more politically engaged citizens" is weak, because the third property of the Internet is relevantly dissimilar to the third property of television (and radio for that matter).

An analogical argument, as already explained, is stronger or weaker to the extent that the evidence in the premises supports the conclusion. No one could reasonably argue that there is not any possibility for the Internet to play a critical role in an era of political reform, because inductive arguments can never show anything with absolute certainty. But even those who make the previously outlined inductive analogical argument about television are not in a strong position, because the two technologies people are comparing have one very significant difference that could have a major bearing on the technologies' roles in our society.

My main point is that we have good reasons to question the inductive strength of any argument that draws an analogy between television and the Internet. We should be skeptical about these arguments. This does not mean that we have reason to believe that the Internet will lead to an era of political reform; what it means is that we do not have good reasons to be cynical about the future of the Internet and our democracy.

Some Encouraging Data

Although many Americans still neglect Net politics the way they neglect politics in general, there is nevertheless increasing interest in Net politics. Signs are that interest will continue to increase. A 2000 Yankelovich/American University poll showed that 29 percent of online Americans (who represented 49 percent of the public) "access information about politics, candidates, and political campaigns" and that 51 percent of the public overall believes that the Internet is a "very important" or "somewhat important" source of election information. Ron Faucheux interprets these findings as an "indication of the potential growth explosion ahead."[7]

A 2000 poll by the Pew Center for the People and the Press reported that one-third of Americans get news from the Internet on a regular basis and that 46 percent of America's youth get news from the Internet at least once per week.[8] The poll also found that regular viewers of television network news have dropped from 60 percent of the public in 1993 to 30 percent in 2000. The poll also showed marked increases in viewer attention to cable television. Michael Kelly interprets this to mean that "customized" news and information—whether from cable television or the Net—is where the action is. "The Internet," he said, "is the coming thing."[9]

A 1999 Democracy Online Project poll, coordinated by Lake, Snell, and Perry and the Tarrance Group, showed that the online electorate wants more information on the following topics: candidate issues and voting records (77 percent); community problems (76 percent); government programs (68 percent); candidate biographies (63 percent); issue and ballot initiatives from nonpartisan sources (63 percent); and voter registration information and polling locations (62 percent). It also found that 75 percent of the online electorate "find candidate information on the Internet very or somewhat accurate."[10] That so many online Americans trust the Net for political information is a very good sign. Compare the 75 percent figure to Americans' trust in the federal government to do the right thing most or all of the time: 21 percent in 1994 (though up to 40 percent by 1998).[11]

With regard to the Internet in general, a 2000 poll commissioned by National Public Radio, the Kaiser Family Foundation, and Harvard University's Kennedy School of Government "shows that people overwhelmingly think that computers and the Internet have made Americans' lives better."[12] There are definite areas of concern, especially regarding inequality (the "digital divide") and content (dangerous online material, including strangers contacting children). But Americans are basically very bullish about the Net.

If you add this encouraging data to the weak arguments about cynicism toward the Net, you should arrive at a place of skepticism, if not cautious optimism: We really do not know how the Internet is going to affect politics and society in the United States. Thus, we should not assume that things will stay the same or that they will get worse.[13] An attitude of cautious optimism seems to be appropriate, as there are many signs that things could be different with the Net. Moreover, an attitude of cautious optimism is much more likely to generate positive change than extremely optimistic or utopian approaches.

Two Misconceptions about Net Politics

In order to replace cynicism with cautious optimism, it will help to remove some additional misconceptions about Internet politics. Two of the main ones are addressed here.

Misconception #1: Net Politics Is Essentially about Campaigns and Elections

The first misconception is that politics is essentially about campaigns and elections. Many citizens believe this because they think that citizenship is essentially about voting. Because citizens see campaigns and elections as the essence of politics, they are inclined to see Net politics in the same way. It is understandable that considerable attention is focused on campaigns and elections during presidential election years, but even in nonelection years, citizens and most journalists still associate Internet politics with campaigns and elections more than anything else.

From the standpoint of citizens' political participation, it is a misconception to think about citizenship in terms of voting or, more generally, in terms of campaigns and elections. Verba, Schlozman, and Brady explain their approach in their massive study on political participation:

> Americans who wish to take part in politics can be active in many ways. Studies of political participation traditionally have begun with—and too often ended with—the vote. Although voting is an important mode of citizen involvement in political life, it is but one of many political acts. In this study we move well beyond the vote to consider a wider range of political acts, including working in and contributing to electoral campaigns and organizations; contacting government officials; attending protests, marches, or demonstrations; working informally with others to solve some community problem; serving without pay on local elected and appointed boards; being active politically through the intermediary voluntary associations; and contributing money to political causes in response to mail solicitations.[14]

The same point applies to Internet politics. Whenever I tell people I am involved in an Internet and politics project, they ask me when voting will be done online. Their next question is about some aspect of election politics. Little interest is shown in the other areas of political participation. So, online voting has a greater presence in the minds of most citizens than other areas of politics.

Misconception #2: The Internet Is Essentially about Information

The second misconception is about the Internet itself. I have argued elsewhere that it is a mistake to assume that the Internet is essentially about providing information and also that it is a mistake to assume that the purpose of providing information is to enable individuals to make decisions.[15] Although it is, of course, true that web sites can and do provide information for individuals to make decisions, the mistake is to assume that this is *all* the Internet does. Donating money online, volunteering for a candidate online, and raising questions to a candidate in an online interactive forum are all examples of online activities that are not best understood as decisions based on information. The Internet is essentially about relationships—interactions between individuals and individuals, individuals and organizations, and organizations and organizations. The relationships can be personal, commercial, or political. The interactive nature of the Net makes these relationships possible. If we think in terms of information and decisions, then we distort the action-oriented nature of this highly interactive medium. We think of the Internet as an encyclopedia of facts rather than a medium that connects people and organizations in a great range of ways.

Consider two reasons why the information/decision model is misleading. First, information that is acquired from the Internet might satisfy a need without leading you to make a decision. For example, you might gain valuable medical information from a web site or a chat room, information that provides emotional relief from some health-related worry. There is no decision to be made after you experience the relief. Not every line on the Internet, indeed not every human utterance, is designed to elicit a decision from someone else.

Second, what is often considered information is not information. A discourse about or from cancer sufferers, although it contains factual claims, is in most cases emotive discourse and not factual or informational discourse. Likewise, requests for campaign volunteers, campaign contributions, and campaign questions are not best regarded as information. A request is not a fact. Neither is an expression of pain. It is a fact that a request is made and that pain is expressed, but making the request and expressing the pain do not state facts about the world.

As Wittgenstein and Austin demonstrated fifty years ago, we do things with words other than report states of affairs about the world.[16] We grossly distort human communication if we group all utterances under the category of descriptive or factual claims. Certainly, numerous moral claims cannot be subsumed under a general category of factual informational discourse without distorting the nature of moral deliberation and moral argument. When every possible human utterance is regarded as information, this narrows our view of the range of capacities that are related to communication.

The Upshot

The upshot of the two misconceptions is as follows: If you think that politics is essentially about campaigns and elections, and if you think that the Internet is essentially about information that is supplied for individuals to make choices, then you probably think that Internet politics is essentially about acquiring information to make choices in elections. Although the (deductive) inference is valid because the conclusion follows logically from the premises, the argument is unsound because both premises are false: Politics is not essentially about campaigns and elections, and the Internet is not essentially about information supplied to individuals in order for them to make choices. As most people tacitly accept these two premises, they are led, quite logically, to conclude that Net politics is essentially about acquiring information to make choices in elections.

Moreover, this leads people to think about citizenship in terms of well-informed or ill-informed voters. Thus they probably infer that Net politics will be successful when we have well-informed voters in the voting booths. Although this may be one of the signs of a successful Internet politics, it would certainly not be the only one, especially if voter turnout does not increase.

It is also worth noting that the very notion of the informed citizen, as Michael Schudson has argued, is largely a product of the progressive era.[17] He distinguishes four models of citizenship that correspond to the founding era, the nineteenth century, the progressive era, and the contemporary period: models (or ideals) of republican virtue, party loyalty, informed citizenship, and rights-conscious citizenship. The informed citizenship model is "the most honored notion of citizenship," but our task today is to seek a synthesis of all four.[18] Schudson's historical, sociological, and moral arguments for why the "informed citizen" notion has been given too much emphasis in our efforts to build a society of good citizens provides additional support for common citizen misconceptions about online politics.

Where Citizens Should Go for Net Political Participation

Conceptually, we have seen that it is easy to think of Net politics as centering around the concept of the well-informed voter and the whole area of election politics. This way of thinking severely limits the possibilities of democratic renewal. Election politics is sure to play an important role in any long-term process of political transformation, but the area of politics that is most likely to hook citizens into the political process is issue politics. Some Internet politics observers have already predicted that the ultimate value of the Net for politics will lie less in candidate campaigns than issue campaigns. The "real revolution" in Internet politics, as Colin Delany puts it, may be in issue advocacy. He writes:

> But most articles about politics and the Internet have missed a part of the story that will linger beyond the periodic frenzy of campaign seasons: organizations and corporations across the country are learning to use the Internet for campaigns about issues rather than about candidates. This could well be the real Internet political revolution: a nonstop online campaign, launched from thousands of sources targeting hundreds of issues across the country and around the world.[19]

Delany explains how the Internet provides organizations with "major advantages over traditional media." A "credible web site" is much cheaper than a professional brochure or a series of television ads. An issue campaign can be launched almost instantly on the Internet, in comparison to the weeks it would take using phones, faxes, and mail. The Net also removes intermediaries like the press from the organization's effort to issue official communications such as press releases, issue papers, and speeches. Likewise, the Internet gives the organization the ability to target potential followers according to interest rather than geographical location.

Issue campaigns occupy 365 days of the year, but candidate campaigns occupy an average of six months every two or four years. Whether the issue is gun safety locks, prescription drug programs, school construction, child care, or elder care, citizens can find opportunities online to make their voices heard. A number of major political protests in the past few years have relied heavily on the Internet, including the Million Mom March (for gun safety) and the IMF/World Bank Protest for Global Justice.

Pam Fielding and Daniel Bennett of E-Advocates explain the core principles of cyberadvocacy in their book, *The Net Effect: How Cyberadvocacy is Changing the Political Landscape*.[20] They discuss a number of cybercampaigns, including the Save the E-Rate campaign, which Fielding led when she was at the National Educational Association. The Center for Democracy and Technology (CDT) has led numerous online campaigns, most notably the Anti-Communications Decency Act campaign (especially with the help of Jonah Seiger and Shabbir Safdir). This campaign included the Paint the Web Black protest when the coalition of organizations and individuals blacked out their web pages after President Clinton signed the Communications Decency Act. CDT's Jerry Berman and Deirdre Mulligan discuss this and other online campaigns in their contribution to this volume.[21]

Jim Buie identifies twenty-two examples of online citizen activism in a recent essay, including efforts launched by citizens without the help of cyberadvocacy firms or interest groups.[22] His examples include Jody Williams's successful cyberadvocacy campaign to ban land mines in eighty-nine countries, the Advocacy Institute's successful cyberadvocacy campaign to block the Smoker's Bill of Rights tour by Phillip Morris, and the Protect Our Heritage Forests campaign to protect the wild forests; this campaign generated 150,000 postcards to Vice President Gore.

Citizens should not underestimate the opportunities for political engagement in issue advocacy campaigns. Moreover, they should not underestimate their opportunities to respond to requests for public opinions about critical issues being considered by federal agencies. Barry Rubin argues that this is the most effective way that citizens are communicating with government today.[23] The possibilities for new coalitions in issue advocacy campaigns are endless when you consider how the Internet facilitates communication among people who would otherwise have difficulty finding each other. In the same way that persons with illnesses can find emotional support in online chat rooms, persons with commitments to social ends can make their connections through the Internet. Even wide generation gaps can be overcome online: there are already interesting examples of younger and older citizens working together, via the Internet, to bring about legislative changes at the local and state levels.[24] As grandmothers are sending instant messages to their grandchildren to keep in touch, so, too, are seniors sending instant messages to students for political purposes. Imagine the possibilities for intergenerational issue advocacy campaigns—grandparents to grandchildren—about such important topics as gun safety, tobacco, and drugs and alcohol.

If citizens go to the Net for issue advocacy politics, then this will surely affect election politics in the future. The polarized politics that E.J. Dionne, Jr. and others have discussed for years could yield to a politics that addresses issues in ways that speak to a new center for American politics.[25] The content of American elections would be improved if citizens bring more content to our issue advocacy campaigns. Issue politics could motor, or indeed "hard drive," this transformation.

Conclusion: Responsibility, Citizenship, and Issue Politics

In concluding, I wish to raise a point about political cynicism that is rarely addressed. It concerns citizen self-deception. Discussions about political cynicism are usually discussed in a vacuum. People talk about Watergate, Vietnam, campaign finance, and character scandals but ignore nonpolitical sources of cynicism. It seems reasonable to speculate that, for many citizens, cynicism about politics is based as much or even more on their cynical feelings about their family relationships and business relationships (say, if they have been victims of adultery, domestic violence, child abuse, desertion, downsizing, and sexual harassment) as it is about the misconduct on the part of politicians and political consultants. Cynicism, like anger, can have many roots.

It is unrealistic to think that the distaste that so many Americans have toward politicians and political consultants is derived entirely or even primarily from the politicians' actions and/or inactions. It is because the media cover the failed efforts and personal misconduct of politicians and political consultants in more detail than that of bosses and spouses and parents that we channel our anger and cynicism toward politicians and political consultants. It is easier to blame people you do not know and will probably never meet than it is to blame people you do know and do not want to confront. Clicking onto political sites and engaging in deliberations with like-minded others would be a fast and effective way to "own" some of the distrust citizens have foisted onto politicians. This would certainly apply to persons whose cynicism is entirely or partly misplaced.

The moral psychology of a nation as large as the United States is a very complicated matter. But any number of important books and social movements have found their origins in key sentiments or insights that were brought to the public, and often these sentiments and insights helped people understand things they felt and believed but could not fully articulate. The time is right for a new era of citizen activism. The Internet, especially with respect to issue politics, could help bring about that era. It could energize offline politics by creating a new offline-online connection.

Yet the technology alone will not move people, and a call for political participation combined with the new technology will not move them either. Citizens armed with self-knowledge, innovative technology, and passion for issues would be in a position to best influence the institutions that tend to ignore their voices.

Moreover, to the extent that government services go online—and the current pace is picking up—citizens could find that many of their frustrations with bureaucratic features about government will diminish. Thus, citizens, with a lot less frustration, would be more likely to think about relating to government in ways that go beyond finding out information and having more efficient relationships with government.

Even individuals who do not have computers and Internet access can get involved at a community site. Many cities provide free computers and Internet service in public libraries and community organizations. The digital divide must be overcome. And major institutional changes, especially corporate changes, are necessary in the United States in order for our society to be free and fair. But even the Divide as it exists today, closing doors to about half of the public, should not stop any American who wants to take a few steps in the direction of becoming a better citizen.

Notes

1. "What Exactly Is a Political Web Site?" PoliticsOnline.com, 23 March 2000 (followed by Weekly Politicker and NetPulse Soundoff), www.politicsonline .com/special/dma.html.

2. The distinction between express advocacy and issue advocacy is implicit in several FEC advisory opinions and a Supreme Court decision. FEC Advisory Opinion 1997–16 (herndon3.sdrdc.com/ao/ao/970016.html) determined that a corporation could not make a list of federal candidate endorsements available on its web site because this would be an example of an express advocacy message directed at the general public. In response to a request by representatives of the George W. Bush campaign, FEC Advisory Opinion 1999–17 (//herndon3.sdrdc .com/ao/ao/9900017.html) determined that if a site does not charge for a link, that link is not considered a contribution. The Federal Election Campaign Act of 1971, 2 USC Sect. 441b, generally prohibits corporate contributions to federal

elections. I am in debt to Neil Reiff and Bob Fertik for very helpful discussions about these points.

3. See Peter Levine's chapter, "Online Campaigning and the Public Interest."

4. The following two essays by Christopher Hunter about online privacy are especially instructive: "Recording the Architecture of Cyberspace Privacy: Why Self-Regulation and Technology Are Not Enough," www.asc.upenn.edu/urs/chunter/p3p.html, and "Privacy Politics and Online Politics: How E-Campaigning Threatens Voter Privacy," www.asc.upenn.edu/usr/chunter/polpriv/political_privacy.html. A revised version was published in the February 2002 edition of *First Monday*, www.firstmonday.dk/issues/issue7_2/hunter/index/html.

5. The television/Internet analogy is discussed by Richard Davis, "Communications Technology and Democracy," in *The Web of Politics: The Internet's Impact on the American Political System* (Oxford: Oxford University Press, 1999), 9–39; and Bruce Bimber, "The Internet and Political Transformation: Populism, Community, and Accelerated Pluralism," *Polity* 31, no. 1 (1998): 133–60. Also available online at www.polsci.ucsb.edu/faculty/bimber/research/transformation.html.

6. Deductive arguments can be valid or invalid and sound or unsound. A sound deductive argument meets two conditions: (1) it has true premises, and (2) it is valid, which basically means that the conclusion follows logically (or necessarily) from the premises.

7. Yankelovich Partners for American University's Center for Congressional and Presidential Studies, *Executive Summary*, 7–8, www.american.edu/campaignconduct/pdfiles/americans_speak_out.pdf. Ron Faucheux's discussion of the poll can be found in "Who Uses the Internet for Election Info?" on Politics/Washingtonpost.com, //washingtonpost.com/wp-=dyn/articles/A36242–2000Jun10.html.

8. Pew Center for the People and the Press, "Internet Sapping Broadcast News Audience: Investors Now Go Online for News Advice," 11 June 2000, www.people-press.org/reports/display.php3?ReportID=36.

9. Michael Kelly, "Network Snooze," *Washington Post*, 14 June 2000, 39(A). Also available online at www.washingtonpost.com/wp-dyn/articles/A53597–2000Jun13.html.

10. Democracy Online Project National Survey, www.democracyonline.org.

11. The NES Guide to Public Opinion and Electoral Behavior, Trust the Federal Government 1958–1998, National Election Studies, Table 5A.1, www.umich.edu/~nes/nesguide/.

12. National Public Radio, the Kaiser Family Foundation, and Harvard University's Kennedy School of Government, *Survey Shows Widespread Enthusiasm for High Technology*, press release, Tuesday, 29 February 2000, 4 P.M. EST.

13. Laura Gurak discusses the prophets of doom in *Persuasion and Privacy in Cyberspace* (New Haven and London: Yale University Press, 1997), 3–4.

14. Sidney Verba, Kay Lehman Schlozman, and Henry E. Brady, *Voice and Equality: Civic Voluntarism in American Politics* (Cambridge, Mass.: Harvard University Press, 1995), 42.

15. David M. Anderson, "The False Assumption about the Internet," *Computers and Society* (March 2000), 8–9.

16. Ludwig Wittgenstein, *The Philosophical Investigations* (Oxford: Blackwell, 1953); and J. L. Austin, *How to Do Things with Words* (Oxford: Oxford University Press, 1962).

17. Michael Schudson, *The Good Citizen* (New York: The Free Press, 1998), 6, 9, 182–85.

18. Schudson, *Citizen*, 9–10, 294–314.

19. *The Real Revolution? Issue Advocacy Campaigning on the Internet*, PoliticalInformation.com, 29 September 1999, www.politicalinformation.com/features.html.

20. Merrifield, VA: E-Advocates Press, 1999.

21. See Jerry Berman and Deirdre Mulligan's chapter, "Digital Grass Roots: Issue Advocacy in the Age of the Internet."

22. Jim Buie, *Think Globally, Act Locally: How the Internet is Changing Advocacy—22 Examples of Citizen Activism Via Computer*, www.us.net/indc/activis.htm.

23. Barry Rubin, *A Citizen's Guide to Politics in America*, 2d ed. (New York: M.E. Sharp, 2000), 228–29.

24. A number of examples were given by witnesses at the final panel ("From K through Grey: Will Online Politics Break Through Generational Barriers?") of the first of three public testimony sessions conducted by the Democracy Online Project's National Task Force, April 17, 2000, //democracyonline.org/taskforce/conferences/1.shtml.

25. E. J. Dionne, Jr., *Why Americans Hate Politics* (New York: Simon and Shuster, 1991).

If Political Fragmentation Is the Problem, Is the Internet the Solution?

3

WILLIAM A. GALSTON

THE THESIS OF THIS CHAPTER may be briefly stated: A central problem—perhaps *the* central problem—of contemporary American politics is the proliferation of single-interest groups and the simultaneous weakening of the institutions and processes needed to balance and integrate the interests these groups represent. And unless current trends are reversed, Internet-mediated politics is more likely to accentuate than to cure this problem.

My argument for this thesis runs as follows:

During the past generation, unfettered individual choice has become an increasingly dominant norm in American culture.

Scholars in a range of disciplines have traced the rise of choice as a core value. Daniel Yankelovich suggests that what he calls the "affluence effect"—the psychology of prosperity that emerged as memories of the Depression faded and as the middle class expanded—has weakened traditional restraint:

> People came to feel that questions of how to live and with whom to live were a matter of individual choice not to be governed by restrictive norms. As a nation, we came to experience the bonds of marriage, family, children, job, community, and country as constraints that were no longer necessary.[1]

In Alan Ehrenhalt's account, the new centrality of individual choice is a key explanation for the transformation of Chicago's neighborhoods since the 1950s.[2] Lawrence Friedman argues that individual choice is the central norm around which the modern American legal system has been restructured.[3] And based on interviews with hundreds of families, Alan Wolfe finds individual choice to be at the heart of the nonjudgmental tolerance that defines middle-class morality in contemporary America.[4]

As individual choice becomes more central, social bonds tend to weaken.

Every student of the choice revolution has found evidence of diminishing bonds. A generation ago, Ralf Dahrendorf offered an influential account of this tension.[5] Yankelovich summarizes the core argument as follows:

> Dahrendorf sees all historic shifts in Western culture as efforts to balance choices and bonds. Choices enhance individualism and personal freedom; bonds strengthen social cohesiveness and stability. In societies where the bonds that link people to one another and to institutions are rigid, the individual's freedom of choice is limited. As people struggle to enlarge their sphere of choice, the bonds that bind them together slacken.[6]

Despite the attractions of individual choice, the desire for attachments is a permanent feature of the human condition.

Although individual human beings vary widely in their tolerance for solitude and desire for community, as a species we are not designed to live alone or in a series of transitory attachments. Much of modern literature (and popular culture, as limned in city-based television shows) traces the movement from the initial exhilaration of shedding strong bonds to the dissatisfactions of life lived without them.

To the extent that expanded choice leads to weaker attachments, therefore, it is bound to trigger an acute sense of loss, expressed in ways ranging from psychological disorders to an intense longing for community. Nonetheless, few Americans are willing to sacrifice the expansive liberty they now enjoy in the name of stronger marriages, neighborhoods, or citizenship. Many Americans regard with horror the prospect of being (as they see it) "trapped" in associations or relationships that no longer fulfill their desires or meet their needs.

This tension between the longing for community and the fear of community constitutes what many Americans experience as the central dilemma of our age; as Wolfe puts it, "how to be an autonomous person and tied together with others at the same time."[7] There is an obvious motivation for reducing this tension as far as possible—that is, for finding ways of living that combine a satisfactory measure of individual autonomy and satisfying social bonds.

The effort to reconcile individual choice and social bonds gives rise to a preference for a mode of association I will call "voluntary community."

This conception of autonomy-compatible community has three defining conditions: entry is by choice; barriers to exit are low; and intracommunity relations are shaped through mutual adjustment rather than authority or coercion. Part of the excitement surrounding the Internet is the possibility it offers for facilitating the formation of these voluntary communities.

Despite the attractions of voluntary community, its rise intensifies existing social and political problems.

In an earlier article of mine, I argue that, judged against the defining features of community, voluntary communities are thin rather than thick and weak rather than strong and are therefore unlikely to fulfill the needs and desires of those who enter them.[8] In this chapter, I now want to focus on another feature of voluntary communities: namely, the tendency of each one to organize around a narrow range of interests in which the members are in broad agreement. I will argue that this feature exacerbates the growing problem of fragmentation (at least regarding domestic issues) in contemporary American politics.

To avoid misunderstanding, let me make it clear that I have no objection to many of the focused associations that the Internet facilitates; quite the reverse. For example, groups organized around specific diseases provide important emotional support and facilitate the rapid location and sharing of information about promising new therapies. Similarly, groups can form around shared hobbies, and the Internet makes possible interactivities that transcend previous barriers of space and time. My point is only that single-interest organizations are more deeply problematic in the contemporary political domain than in other aspects of our social and associational life.

Voluntary communities tend to be homogeneous.

When given a choice, most people tend to associate with others who are like themselves in the respects they regard as important. Above a relatively low threshold, most people experience deep differences as dissonant and unpleasant. Even when these differences need not be reconciled through explicit collective decisions, they suffuse the shared social space and reduce its appeal for many denizens. To be sure, many people experience differences in food, culture, and even opinion as stimulating . . . so long as they can sample the differences and leave when they choose. For most people, diversity is a nice place to visit, but they don't really want to live there.[9]

Because Internet communities are voluntary, they are more likely to be homogeneous rather than heterogeneous, and group homogeneity can have negative consequences for society as a whole.

In an important theoretical paper, Marshall Van Alstyne and Erik Brynjolfsson show how the Internet can translate even weak preferences for those like oneself into homogeneous subgroups whose internal interactions far exceed cross-group communications, a condition they term "cyberbalkanization." Left unchecked, cyberbalkanization can yield results that are economically efficient (in the sense that no individual can be made better off by switching from more focused to less focused association) but socially suboptimal. For example, the growth of hyperspecialized subcommunities can slow the growth of scientific knowledge, which depends on exchanging of information and theoretical perspectives across group boundaries.[10]

Bruce Bimber suggests that the Internet's probable effect will be the intensification of group-centered politics, which he terms "accelerated pluralism." His argument rests on two empirical premises: first, that the Internet will not alter the fact that most people are highly selective in their attention to issues and information; and second, that the Internet lowers the costs of locating, organizing, and mobilizing communities of like-minded individuals. On the one hand, this later development may be described as the "democratization" of group politics, as lowered transaction costs increase the organizational opportunities of resource-poor groups. On the other hand, accelerated pluralism decreases political coherence and stability and intensifies fragmentation as focused "issue publics" form for transitory purposes, exert single-issue pressure on the political system, and then dissolve. In the process, the power of more traditional public and voluntary sector institutions that currently enjoy some stability through time and work to integrate (or at least broker among) diverse preferences is likely to erode.[11]

The rise of homogeneous communities tends not only to decrease intergroup community and increase political fragmentation, but it also tends to exacerbate the difficulty of reconciling diverse interests and world views. Cass Sunstein summarizes a wide range of empirical studies, conducted in more than a dozen nations, that point toward a common conclusion: a group of like-minded people who engage in discussion with one another are likely to adopt more extreme rather than more moderate variants of the group's shared beliefs. And it turns out that particularly high levels of polarization occur when group members meet anonymously—which is precisely what the Internet permits. By contrast, face-to-face deliberation within heterogeneous groups is more likely to yield a moderation of views all around, or at least a willingness to listen to evidence and arguments and to alter one's considered judgments.[12]

To be sure, anonymity can also foster heterogeneity by reducing the salience of the differences that hinder the formation of traditional groups. Online groups united by shared interests may be remarkably diverse in their ethnic, religious, class, and age composition, and the effects of differences (of gender, for example) that frequently skew active participation can be reduced.

Still, it is hard to see how this anonymous heterogeneity can yield stronger bonds across lines of division unless diverse individuals eventually reveal their identities to one another—that is, unless they are willing to forego the comforts of homogeneity. It is a matter of utmost importance for citizens in a diverse society to understand that they can have something important in common, and can work, with others who are unlike them in important respects. For this lesson to be learned, group members must know one another in their differences as well as their commonalities. From this perspective, one might hypothesize that a socially optimal mix would be one of anonymous and identity-revealing political interactions. To the extent that virtual communities not only supplement but actually replace attachments to geographical communities, however, societies are less likely to reap the advantages of this optimal mix.[13]

The multiplication of single-interest groups is especially damaging at a time when the forces of fragmentation in American politics are more powerful than are the sources of integration across issues and interests.

During the past generation, single-interest groups have become a dominant feature of the American political landscape. Jonathan Rauch has documented the extraordinary growth of advocacy organizations, especially those created to push focused agendas through Washington-based lobbying.[14] (Examples of such groups in an online contest may be seen in chapters 6 and 7 of this book.)

At the same time as these single-interest groups have grown, long-standing sources of integration across issues and interests have weakened. Three developments are of particular importance:

1. As Theda Skocpol has shown, broad-based civil associations that assemble individuals across class lines and that link states and localities with the national political dialogue have weakened while narrower organizations with top-down structures have expanded in influence.[15]
2. Network broadcasting has lost market share to the proliferation of smaller-audience niche alternatives ("narrowcasting"). This is part of a larger trend in which what Andrew Shapiro calls "general interest intermediaries" are losing ground to media that allow individuals to design their own mix of information and entertainment.[16] This is the sociopolitical equivalent of the Internet-driven processes of disintermediation so clearly visible in financial markets.
3. As political parties have become more homogeneous internally, they have become less able to reach accommodations across partisan lines. And as a plebiscitary nomination process has displaced the prior system of brokered representative institutions, the capacity of political parties to conduct internal deliberations has diminished.

It may seem paradoxical that my analysis focuses on the proliferation of single-interest groups as the principal problem of modern

American politics. After all, it was James Madison who famously identified the multiplication of "factions" as a key guarantor of individual rights and liberties. But Madison was equally cognizant of the need to reach agreements across factional differences in order to promote the common good, and he pointed to two features of the new constitutional order that he hoped would serve that purpose. First, he argued that electoral processes would tend to select individuals whose "enlightened views and virtuous sentiments" would make them more likely and more able to identify the public good through reasoned deliberation than would the people themselves acting directly. Second, he argued that although every constitutional institution drew its legitimate authority directly or indirectly from the people, many of those institutions were designed to be buffered against popular pressure and thus against the baneful influence of factions on public decision making.

Historians debate whether these Madisonian processes of filtration and insulation were ever adequate to their task. Whatever may have been true two centuries ago, it is hard to maintain that these two processes can suffice in modern circumstances. One may wonder whether the traits of mind and character needed to wage and win today's elections are congruent with the wisdom and virtue Madison hoped electoral competition would single out. Post-Madisonian constitutional developments—the rise of political parties, the evisceration of the electoral college as a deliberative body, and direct election of senators, among others—have increased direct popular influence over key institutions and have lowered barriers to factional influences in the policy process.

If fragmentation is a central problem of contemporary American politics, then thinkers and policy makers—including Internet architects—must think harder about how existing institutions can be reformed (or new ones created) to deliberate on, or at least strike a reasonable balance among, competing interests and values.

It is now fashionable to denigrate the institutions of our official politics, starting with the Congress. If my analysis is correct—if longstanding unofficial mechanisms of political integration have weakened—then this stance has it exactly backwards. In current circumstances, official institutions are more important than ever as the principal venues within which competing interests and values must somehow be brought together into a course of common action.

When the American people reach broad agreement on what needs to be done, as they did about the Welfare system in the 1990s and as they appear to be doing about prescription drugs today, then official institutions can usually find ways to respond. But when the people are divided or have not focused on an issue and decisions nonetheless must be made (e.g., on telecommunications legislation), we must look for new ways of reducing the impact of single-interest groups on legislation and regulation while ensuring that these groups continue to enjoy a fair chance of expressing their views.

For example, more intensive press scrutiny of important but virtually invisible steps in legislative and regulatory processes would be a good start. No doubt the leaders of media organizations would resist this on the grounds that the people are not very interested in most legislative and regulatory outcomes, let alone the tedious and unsightly battles that produce them. To this we must reply: Maybe not, but part of your responsibility is to remember the distinction between what the people say they want and what they need for the exercise of informed citizenship. What the people do with the information is up to them, but if market-driven considerations lead you to edit it out in advance, the people will never have the chance to decide for themselves. And it is not enough to say that the information is available on, say, cable channels with minute ratings. General-purpose intermediaries still send important signals about what matters, and they have some responsibility to exercise their power in the public interest. If they refuse to do even the basics—for example, televising important debates during presidential primaries—then perhaps we must seek constitutionally appropriate ways of mandating such coverage.

As I indicated earlier in this chapter, we must also use our imaginations to think of new ways to enlist the Internet on the side of political integration. Let me be clear about the central presupposition of this quest: If individual choice—on the Internet as well as elsewhere—leads to the formation of voluntary communities, if these communities are homogeneous in crucial respects, and if this homogeneity is part of the overall problem of social and political fragmentation, then effective responses are likely to require some restrictions on individual choice.

These limitations need not, and probably should not, be imposed directly on individual choosers; rather, they can be built into the background architecture of the information system. For example, Andrew Chin and Cass Sunstein propose that the current legislative "must carry" doctrine mandated for cable systems should be extended to the Internet. Under this proposal, especially popular web sites would be required to link to a selection of sites that draw the public's attention to public issues and to increase the information they possess.[17] No one would be forced to visit these public interest sites, but at least the chances for average citizens to know about them would increase.

I am not an expert on Internet design. But those who are must set aside the cyberlibertarian fantasy that unfettered choice always is conducive to the long-term welfare of the community as a whole. Neoclassical economists have persuasively analyzed a range of "market failures." It is time for the framers of the constitution for our information future to take these insights seriously in their own revolutionary domain, to consider the peril as well as the promise of unrestricted choice on the Internet, and—consistent with our constitutional traditions—to find new ways of enlisting the Internet in the cause of informed citizenship and the common good.

Notes

1. Daniel Yankelovich, "How Changes in the Economy Are Reshaping American Values," in *Values and Public Policy*, ed. Henry J. Aaron, Thomas E. Mann, and Timothy Taylor (Washington, D.C.: Brookings, 1994), 20.

2. Alan Ehrenhalt, *The Lost City: Discovering the Forgotten Virtues of Community in the Chicago of the 1950s* (New York: Basic Books, 1995), chaps. 12 and 13.

3. Lawrence Friedman, *The Republic of Choice: Law, Authority, and Culture* (Cambridge, MA: Harvard, 1990).

4. Alan Wolfe, *One Nation, After All* (New York: Viking, 1998).

5. Ralf Dahrendorf, *Life Chances: Approaches to Social and Political Theory* (London: Weidenfeld and Nicolson, 1979).

6. Yankelovich, "How Changes in the Economy Are Reshaping American Values," 20.

7. Wolfe, *One Nation, After All*, 132.

8. William A. Galston, "(How) Does the Internet Affect Community? Some Speculations in Search of Evidence," in *democracy.com? Governance in a Networked World*, ed. Elaine Ciulla Kamarck and Joseph S. Nye, Jr. (Hollis, N.H.: Hollis Publishing, 1999). Portions of chapter 3 were adapted from this essay.

9. Even when individuals and groups express a general preference for diversity, their divergent understandings of diversity in practice can yield homogeneity. For example, most African Americans define an integrated neighborhood as one populated by Blacks and Whites in roughly equal numbers, but most Whites define an integrated neighborhood as one in which African Americans constitute roughly their share of the national population—that is, 12 percent. The interaction of these competing definitions tends to produce racially homogeneous neighborhoods.

10. Marshall Van Alstyne and Erik Brynjolfsson, *Electronic Communities: Global Village of Cyberbalkans?* (Cambridge: MIT Sloan School, 1997).

11. Bruce Bimber, "The Internet and Political Transformation: Populism, Community, and Accelerated Pluralism," *Polity* 31, no.1 (Fall 1998): 133–60.

12. Cass Sunstein, *Republic.Com* (Princeton, N.J.: Princeton University Press, 2001), chap. 3.

13. For an illuminating discussion on this point, I am indebted to my fellow symposiasts at the meeting on digital democracy organized by the National Research Council (June 1–2, 2000, Washington, D.C.).

14. Jonathan Rauch, *Demosclerosis: The Silent Killer of American Government* (New York: Times Books, 1994).

15. Theda Skocpol, "Advocates without Members: The Recent Transformation of American Civic Life," in *Civic Engagement in American Democracy,* ed. Theda Skocpol and Morris P. Fiorina (Washington, D.C.: Brookings, 1999).

16. Andrew L. Shapiro, *The Control Revolution: How the Internet Is Putting Individuals in Charge and Changing the World We Know* (New York: Public Affairs, 1999).

17. Sunstein, *Republic.Com,* page 187, quoting Andrew Chin, "Making the World Wide Web Safe for Democracy," 19 *Hastings Communications/Entertainment Law Journal* 309 (1997).

THE CURRENT STATE OF
ONLINE POLITICS

Online Campaigning and the Public Interest   4

PETER LEVINE

TECHNOLOGICAL DETERMINISTS expect the Internet to remake politics in its own image, just as it is transforming business and education. They expect to see candidates engaging in direct, unfiltered, two-way communications with citizens. They predict that entrenched incumbents will soon face formidable challenges from novices, outsiders, and insurgents armed only with listservs and web pages. They imagine that the electorate will become more engaged and informed than ever before, thanks to the massive store of free information that the Internet provides. And they hope that the World Wide Web will make good arguments, rather than money or power, prevail in politics. "The Internet is by nature a democratic medium," according to Jonah Seiger, cofounder of Mindshare Internet Campaigns, an online political strategy firm. "Every single user is a publisher, limited not by resources, but only by whether they have a compelling message."[1]

I offer no wholesale refutation of technological determinism. However, it is generally wise to consider not only what a technology can accomplish, but also what incentives and objectives motivate the people who use it. In the political arena, the major players' main goals—winning elections, passing legislation, and influencing the government—predate the Internet and will continue to shape its use. It is also important to examine how any new technology has actually been employed so far, keeping in mind its potential for change and reform. The tentative conclusions of this chapter are based on several dozen well-regarded campaign web sites from the 1998 and 2000 campaigns as well as from a statistical analysis of 554 sites conducted by Elaine Kamarck of Harvard University. Kamarck's study group looked at every site established by a candidate for the U.S. House or Senate, or for state governor, in 1998.[2]

Politicians, parties, and consultants increasingly believe that establishing an Internet presence may help them to win. But the public also has interests that campaigns ought to serve. The question is whether political web sites promote, or are likely in the future to promote, several specific public goods.

Transmitting Information

The most obvious public good that campaigns can serve is to transmit information to voters who already possess settled political preferences. Citizens who know what ideology or what kind of leader they favor need facts to help them decide whom to support. Useful guidance can come from candidates' official statements and campaign behavior, from news coverage and editorial commentary, and from endorsements. At the same time, the candidates' campaign promises represent a kind of contract with the voters, enforceable at the next election. Thus, promoting accountability and providing information are two closely linked public functions.

The Harvard study found information about issues and/or found candidates' biographies on 81 percent of campaign web sites. The sites that I explored presented this information in an abbreviated—almost coded—fashion, so as to impress people who already knew where they stood on such complex topics as "social promotion," "a woman's right to choose" (the word abortion is usually omitted), or a "balanced-budget amendment." I found few, if any, efforts to explain concepts or to change people's minds.

Representative Mark Neumann, who ran for the Senate in 1998, had a web site that was impressively substantive. Using several graphs, he argued that his budget plan would wipe out the federal debt by 2026, which then seemed an ambitious goal. But he didn't try to persuade visitors to his site that debt reduction was more important than other goals, nor did he define such esoteric terms as "Gramm-Rudman" that would mystify most Americans. ("Gramm-Rudman" refers to legislation that automatically cut federal spending if Congress exceeded specific targets.)

Steve Clift of Minnesota E-Democracy argues that "the Net is best used at this stage . . . to *assemble and coordinate*, not to *persuade*."[3] In short, people who had already developed political preferences could gain useful information from campaign web pages, assuming that they had access to the Internet. But the value of such information should not be exaggerated. Only motivated voters would benefit from it, and they could easily obtain the same data from other sources. A conscientious voter could even skip campaign materials altogether and rely instead on the "issue grids" and voter guides that are now printed by many newspapers and by the League of Women Voters. On the other hand, it is not always safe to trust intermediaries to be fair and accurate, and it can be illuminating when candidates present their issues in their own way, with their own choices of emphasis and rhetoric.

The Internet has potential advantages for this kind of communication. For one thing, messages arrive in a medium that is well suited to research. If a candidate says on her web page that she will hire 75,000 new public school teachers, you can click the mouse a few times and find out what her opponent would do, what the teachers' union thinks about this, how much money teachers are paid, and how many teachers are already employed in your state. A television commercial might prompt similar questions in your mind, but you would have to leave the television to get answers. Some campaign web sites allow visitors to e-mail questions, so that citizens can ask about issues of special concern to themselves. But again, this is not an advance over toll-free telephone numbers, which people can also call with comments and questions. Exchanges with voters are ultimately limited in both forums by shortages of qualified personnel and of time.

Mobilizing Voters

As a method of presenting candidates' positions, résumés, and campaign pledges to motivated voters, the Internet seems useful, although hardly revolutionary. But another function of campaigns is to encourage political participation. Although poll taxes have been abolished, voting still requires expenditures of time and effort. Most people do not vote unless someone reduces the effort of participation by providing them with free facts about the candidates' agendas and résumés, about how to register, and about where to vote.

Campaign rhetoric can be motivating, too. Dan Lungren's 1998 web page announced: "Dear California voter, my campaign for governor is for the people of this state—not for the expensive consultants and high priced politicos who have become a fixture in California campaigns." The purpose of this statement was to persuade visitors to get involved.

But something has gone wrong with mobilization in the United States, for more than one-half of American adults sat out the 1996 election, the worst showing in a presidential year since 1924,[4] and the 1998 congressional races set an all-time record for the number of eligible citizens who stayed home (111 million people).[5] Steven Rosenstone and John Mark Hansen attribute 54 percent of the change in turnout between the 1960s and the 1980s to a decline in mobilization.[6] By this they mean a weakening of parties, a decrease in the frequency of competitive campaigns, the rising demands on voters because of primary elections, and a dearth of social movements. I would also emphasize the change in the mechanics of campaigns. Until the 1960s, a great deal of labor and local knowledge was required to arrange campaign events, to visit people on their front porches, to canvass voters, and to address and stuff mailings. Most of this work was done by parties, which therefore had an interest in recruiting potential workers—even among the young, the poor, and the newest of immigrants. But today's campaigns are high-tech. They demand specialized skills and money, not ordinary labor or local knowledge, and more than 50 percent of their funds comes from 1 percent of the population. Moreover, they are able to target their messages to a narrow group: likely but undecided voters. Those who are asked to participate in politics tend to comply, but modern campaigns have no reason to contact most people.[7]

Perhaps campaign web sites will cheaply reach some Americans who are not influenced by other media: those who don't read newspapers or watch the television news but who happen to enjoy surfing the Internet.[8] According to a Pew poll, only one in twenty Internet users visited the web site of a candidate or campaign in 1998,[9] but presumably the use of such sites will grow as the percentage of campaigns with worthwhile web pages increases. And the Internet can certainly be used for mobilization efforts. In 1998, half of all campaign web sites allowed visitors to sign up for conventional volunteering. Between 5 and 6 percent of the sites also provided opportunities to conduct volunteer activities on the Internet such as sending e-mail to friends, telling people how to register, or providing links to official voter registration offices.[10] In 2000, Senator Bill Bradley recruited 100,000 volunteers through his presidential campaign web site, and 142,000 people signed up to receive daily e-mail briefings from the John McCain campaign—briefings that often included specific "calls to action." Visitors who join e-mail lists can be quickly and inexpensively told about local events, asked to disseminate information, given sample letters to send to the newspaper, and otherwise encouraged to participate. The Bradley campaign even created a web page to train novices to perform one of the more difficult modern civic acts, participating in a caucus. So some increase in mobilization could occur as a result of Internet politics.[11]

However, campaign sites may have the opposite effect, exacerbating current trends toward a narrow electorate. The medium is well suited for targeting messages to motivated interest groups and for raising money from wealthy donors.[12] Senator Kit Bond's 1998 web page offered a taste of what mobilization and participation can mean in modern campaigns. Visitors were invited to join the Bond Senate Foundation, whose benefits included complimentary tickets to events in their areas, special priority seating at events, campaign briefings, a broadcast fax newsletter, special photo opportunities, and a Bond Senate Foundation lapel pin. The membership requirements were very simple: $2,000.

Promoting Deliberation

Another public purpose of campaigns is to help people to develop opinions about policy questions that they haven't resolved in their own minds or perhaps haven't even considered before. In their quest for office, candidates broach novel topics, answer pointed questions from reporters and activists, and attack each other's positions. This discourse can prompt citizens to form opinions. Voters and candidates may even improve their positions and values because of the campaign debate. By listening to others and hearing alternative views, people may modify their political positions or acknowledge other people's pressing needs. And they may drop views that are shown to be flatly false or impossible. As John Dewey wrote:

> The ballot is, as often said, a substitute for bullets. But what is more significant is that counting of heads compels prior recourse to methods of discussion, consultation, and persuasion, while the essence of appeal to force is to cut short resort to such methods. . . . The strongest point to be made in behalf of even such rudimentary political forms as democracy

has already attained—popular voting, majority rule, and so on—is that to some extent they involve a consultation and discussion which uncover social needs and troubles.[13]

A web page that merely lists campaign positions will not promote consultation and discussion of the type that might generate and improve public opinion. Nor will it do any harm. It may at least assist reporters who want to write substantive and informative articles about issues that the candidates have raised. To a large extent, web pages seem to have become an inexpensive form of press release.

The Internet's potential for interactivity holds some promise for deliberation. But although Kamarck's group searched for the web sites of 1,296 candidates, they found only two "fully interactive" web sites in the 1998 campaign. One of these, established by Pennsylvania gubernatorial candidate Tom Ridge, had vanished by the time I began writing this chapter in the spring of 1999. The other one was impressive. Tom Campbell, a Silicon Valley politician, used his web page to present an archive of voters' questions along with his own lengthy, substantive answers, categorized by topic. He continued this practice when he ran for the Senate in 2000, although he began to select five questions per day to answer instead of attempting to handle every query. Some of his exchanges with voters were strikingly substantive: the equivalent of published academic discourse. As visitors could review other people's dialogues with the candidate, Campbell's web site did more than show people where he stood on issues; they also helped voters to form or change opinions.

In this case, the technology of the Internet—its capacity for inexpensive data storage, wide dissemination, and electronic searching—seems genuinely valuable. Without a web page, Campbell could not easily have made his whole correspondence available to the public. On the other hand, the salient fact is that 99.85 percent of candidates for governor or federal office did *not* have fully interactive web pages in 1998, as the Kamarck study showed. In 2000, presidential candidate Al Gore established an "interactive town hall"—in other words, an archive of voters' questions and of answers from the candidate. But unlike Campbell, who saved every question that he received on his 1998 web page, Gore's campaign posted just a few exchanges that presented the Gore agenda in a positive light. The voters' questions that became part of the online record were mostly softballs: "A few years ago, I heard you say that you would work to reinvent the government. Please explain what reinvent the government means and what you did to accomplish it."[14] In short, Gore's virtual town hall was hardly different from the position papers that presidential candidates now post on their web pages.

In general, candidates do not benefit from genuine, public, open-ended deliberation with voters. Imagine two tactics for getting elected. One is to approach citizens who disagree with you about various issues, attempting to persuade each one to change his or her mind. This is the method that a truly deliberative candidate would employ. At the opposite extreme, you could poll likely voters in your district for an issue about which a majority already agreed with you and disagreed with your opponent. You would then hammer away at that issue and try not to lose focus. Clearly this is an effective tactic, but it can fail if someone engages you in an open-ended, complex discussion of issues that you didn't choose.

Candidates do deliberate and foster deliberation among citizens, when necessary. For instance, they are sometimes asked unavoidable questions in face-to-face situations or during live debates. But these are dangerous situations, and normally politicians don't want to preserve everything that happens there in searchable online databases. Lynn Reed, who designed Bradley's 2000 presidential campaign web site, said, "I'm a political consultant, and the supreme law of political consulting is message consistency."[15] If you happen to be an extreme ideologue, then you may be able to answer every voter's questions without clouding your consistent overall campaign message. As for Tom Campbell, his message was his own personality as a man who thrived on intellectual exchange. But most candidates find that the fewer unplanned topics they discuss on the public record, the better.

Some observers argue that substantive interaction with candidates will occur online because Web users will demand it. Interaction and discussion are hallmarks of cyberspace, and users are discriminating consumers. W. Russell Neuman of the Annenberg School for Communication writes:

> Online voters know their medium well and are easily offended when content is simply shoveled over from other media. The Web, after all, is a fundamentally two-way medium. Web-savvy citizens want the capacity to search and

navigate a web site to find those issues and ideas of special interest. They want to be in the driver's seat, not in the audience. They want dialogue.

Voters understand fully that candidates don't have the time to respond to every e-mail, but they want to see evidence of dialogue, answers to voter queries, occasional online town meetings, the capacity to locate details on issues which don't fit into the strictures of daily newspaper or television coverage. Newspapers and TV are media of immediacy. The Internet taps immediacy too. But the Internet has the capacity to be a medium of record, rich in detail, nuance, and background information not otherwise available.[16]

Perhaps it is no coincidence that Tom Campbell represents the nation's most computer-savvy House district, for he has responded to precisely the values that Neuman describes. In 1998, Campbell's web page announced: "As a representative of Silicon Valley, I understand the importance of the Internet as a means of providing substantive information and facilitating communication." We might expect that as soon as the rest of the country attains the 1998 computer competence of Northern Californians, all campaigns will look like Campbell's. But this will happen only if public demand drives campaign strategy. There are certainly cases when public preferences do not matter very much; for instance, although Americans abhor negative advertising, bitter attacks remain ubiquitous in modern politics. Similarly, the risks of allowing true online interaction may well outweigh the benefits for most campaigns. If both major-party candidates avoid deliberation, then neither one can be punished by dissatisfied voters. And if the result of shallow campaigning is low turnout among Internet users, one candidate will nevertheless be elected.

Campaigns are zero-sum games. The point is not to maximize your support, but to receive at least 50 percent of the vote plus one. It is often easier to drive potential voters away from the opposition than to convert people to your own side, especially given some voters' high levels of distrust for politics. (The same is not true in commercial markets, where an exchange of scurrilous attacks would simply drive down overall demand.) Certainly, politicians would like to engage in high-minded and dignified campaigns that restored public trust—as long as they won. In short, political campaigns have some features of what rational-choice theorists call the "Prisoner's Dilemma": a situation that encourages both sides to choose strategies that generate a poor result for all. As often as not, the bad drives out the good.

Thus, we should be concerned about the Internet's potential for particularly disreputable campaign tactics. Spurious sites could be created that purported to represent a candidate but whose real purpose was to undermine the campaign. Unsolicited e-mails (spam) could be used to annoy potential voters and could be falsely attributed to an opponent. Anonymous sites could be established to make unsubstantiated charges and to spread rumors. Even without resorting to anonymity, a campaign could send false information to selected voters and thereby avoid press scrutiny, especially if it acted close to Election Day. Factual claims on web pages could be backed up with links to misleading or biased sites. At the very least, campaigns could innocently cite some of the many errors that circulate in cyberspace.

Money Matters

Even if the Internet does not force campaigns to provide public goods, it might at least save them money. Jesse Ventura's 1998 Minnesota gubernatorial campaign claims to have set up its impressive and effective site for $200. Therefore, one might hope that candidates who lacked access to broadcast and print media would be able to present their ideas on the World Wide Web. Furthermore, insurgents who attract positive publicity would be able to raise money efficiently online from small donors, whereas they could never afford the costs of direct mail solicitations. During the 2000 presidential primaries, Senator McCain raised $6.4 million online; his fundraising pace reached $10,000 *per hour* immediately after his victory in New Hampshire.[17] (For more on the regulation of online fundraising, see chapter 5.)

Stories like this suggest that the Internet may make politicians less beholden to the wealthy interests that currently finance successful campaigns. Because these donors represent a narrow slice of the population, they promote a certain homogeneity of issues and philosophies. Reducing their influence might increase voters' choice and so make government more representative. However, Kamarck's study found that minor-party candidates made less use of the Internet in 1998 than major-party candidates did.[18] Merely putting up a web page is not very effective unless you can direct eligible voters to it, and so far that seems to require broadcast advertising, mailings, and press coverage. Besides, truly effective web pages are not as inexpensive as the Ventura example indicates. McCain itemized a total of $515,714 for his Internet expenses during the 2000 presidential campaign, and this figure presumably did not include salary and overhead funds for his web page. Bradley spent $351,101 for Internet service and consulting.[19] Although both candidates used the Internet effectively, both were ultimately defeated by better-funded opponents.

Even if the Internet does substantially cut costs and reduce the importance of campaign money, it also has great potential for linking politicians to wealthy national constituencies. As a means of reaching average voters in one's own district, the Web is inexpensive but inefficient, because many of the people who encounter a campaign site may live in another state or country. But as a means of advertising the fact that a candidate supports tort reform or cable television deregulation, the Internet is ideal. I can imagine an executive in the widget industry searching the Web for "candidate AND widget AND regulation," and then mailing some checks. So the Internet may actually increase the role of wealthy interests.

Changing the Incentives

It is possible to alter the pressures that motivate and constrain political candidates. Campaign finance reform would help. Not only would public subsidies reduce the influence of wealthy contributors and make fundraising less time-consuming, but some of the public funds could be reserved for constructive purposes such as minute-long television commercials, mass mailings, get-out-and-vote drives, and broadcast debates. Then candidates would be encouraged to inform and mobilize voters, if not to deliberate with them. Meanwhile, the press could improve the way that it covers campaigns, moving from horse-race coverage that predicts who will win to issue-based reporting that helps voters decide whom to support. Parties could be strengthened and turned to more productive purposes. States and not-for-profits could more frequently distribute voter guides, host debates, promote civic education, and create forums for deliberation—including ones on the Internet.[20] If we achieved some of these reforms, then the World Wide Web would be a valuable tool in the hands of well-motivated candidates.[21]

It would be especially useful to ask all candidates the same specific questions, juxtapose their replies, and give them opportunities in further exchanges to debate what they have written. This kind of interaction makes campaigns serve citizens, not candidates. When prominent independent newspapers, such as the *Charlotte* (North Carolina) *Observer*, publish candidates' statements, campaigns often feel compelled to participate, because otherwise blank spaces will appear beside their names; some independent, Web-based organizations are experimenting with similar formats. For instance:

- The Democracy Network (www.dnet.org) attempts to provide an issue grid for every race across the country. Voters can find relevant pages by providing their zip codes. The political philosopher Dennis Thompson mentions DNet as a paradigm of those sites that "welcome diverse opinions from all citizens, and set a tone that encourages participants to respect the views of others, and to regard politics as an activity that promotes not only factional but also public interests."[22] However, as of May 2000, most candidates had not submitted statements to the DNet voter grids for the 2000 election. Perhaps they calculated that if they wrote something and it proved controversial, then the press, their opponents, or hostile political groups might publicize their answers. The risk of alienating visitors by not participating may have seemed comparatively small, as few voters would see the DNet grids. In contrast, conventional newspapers have enough market share that they can effectively compel candidates to participate.
- Project Vote Smart (www.vote-smart.org) posts candidates' answers to the National Political Awareness Test (NPAT) along with biographies, campaign finance data, and much other information. NPAT asks politicians which of more than 200 specific policies they support. The NPAT results are potentially very helpful to voters who want information about candidates' positions. However, the questionnaire format does not promote deliberation, because candidates offer no reasons for their views.
- Debate America (www.debateamerica.org) presents elaborate debates on important matters of public policy—either national issues or questions specific to the participating communities. The participants include famous intellectuals and experts. There is

also a mechanism that anyone can use to begin a debate of his or her own. The site says: "National candidates often speak in generalities, or talk about issues in ways that don't address the specifics of the communities in which we live. Debate America provides citizens with space and easy-to-use tools to raise, think about, and discuss issues in terms that reflect the concerns of their communities across the country." This site could help foster deliberation, although it does not promise any of the other public goods analyzed earlier in this chapter.

- In addition to a candidate database and other features, GoVote .com (www.govote.com) offers an online quiz that tells participants "which [presidential] candidate best matches [their] views"; it also lets participants know whether they should think of themselves as liberals, conservatives, or libertarians. This format could be expanded to cover more than presidential elections. But most of the current quiz questions are highly simplistic. For instance, visitors are asked whether they support "Foreign aid to Russia, Israel, and others," as if a citizen would have one opinion about all forms of aid to all countries, from Israel to Sierra Leone.

- SpeakOut.com (www.speakout.com, reached via the GoVote.com portal) offers a "candidate selector" somewhat like the GoVote quiz. SpeakOut also polls visitors on issues and sends the results to politicians; it hosts live debates; and it offers short statements on both sides of many public issues, presumably to enlighten undecided citizens. These statements are billed as being better than "thirty-second news stories" that "don't give enough information," and also as being preferable to newspapers and magazines, which "can give you too much data on subjects you don't care about."

- AARP (formerly the American Association for Retired Persons) provided information about all the federal candidates in 2000 who were seeking to represent any zip code, including links to their web pages (via www.aarp.org/election2000/). Through a branch called BeAVoter.org, AARP also currently provides online voter registration.

- Vote.com (www.vote.com) encourages visitors to choose between two contrasting ten-word positions on a leading issue of the day. Each position is explained by a short paragraph, headed "the facts." Vote.com promises: "When you vote on a topic listed on our site, we'll send an immediate e-mail to significant decision makers like your congressional representative, your senators, and the president telling them how you feel."

Some of these sites clearly serve useful public purposes. At least they reduce the cost of identifying the upcoming elections in one's own district, thereby making it slightly easier to participate. But the worst of the sites make political debate crude and visceral, reducing participation and expression to fairly meaningless mouse clicks.

At first glance, it appears that the latter category can do no harm, because there is room in cyberspace for countless projects. Good citizens will seek out good sites, and those who prefer Vote.com probably wouldn't have participated at all without it. But this view of the Internet as a free and unlimited space overlooks shortages of capital and publicity. It costs a great deal of money to create and advertise an appealing, interactive site that can reliably handle heavy traffic. Merely posting information does not guarantee that anyone will find it, especially as some of the major search engines are highly selective: they either focus on popular culture or else charge sites to be listed.[23] For example, none of the participants in a 1999 New Hampshire focus group had heard of DNet or knew how to find it.[24]

David Chiu, a cofounder of GrassRoots.com, explained that his organization formed as a commercial enterprise because it wouldn't have been able to raise adequate funds as a charity. GrassRoots.com then purchased DNet in February 2000.[25] Leaders of the competing political dot-coms expect the market to consolidate further once a few companies have found a profitable business model. Meanwhile, Richard Kimball, executive director of the nonprofit Project Vote Smart, fears that if any firms "become commercially viable, they will become predominant and alone in the field."[26] Once a commercial enterprise duplicates the Project Vote Smart database, the latter will be unable to attract donations.

In theory, a business or a lobbying organization could produce a nonpartisan, substantive, interactive, reliable, and serious political web page that served public interests. But there are grounds for skepticism. First, businesses and lobbies have political agendas that could color their presentation of campaigns and issues. AARP, for instance, provides Election Issue Briefs that are just a few clicks away from its candidate database. These briefs are perfectly respectable, but they present

AARP's point of view. On the other hand, there is hardly any organization without an agenda, and some web sites may choose to build reputations for reliability and trustworthiness by rigorously separating their editorial decisions from their political agendas, just as the best newspapers have done.

A deeper problem is that all commercial firms must settle conflicts between profits and civic values in favor of profits. Nonprofit groups can, on the other hand, pursue their own understandings of the public's interests and obligations. For instance, Debate America structures its site so that "citizens can raise and debate issues of local concern in a thoughtful, respectful manner via the Internet." It emphasizes sober, mostly local issues that might attract less interest—and fewer visitors—than the sensational topics debated on Vote.com. As for Project Vote Smart, it is careful to present information about *every* candidate, even fringe ones. These conceptions of the public good are subject to debate, and the projects' administrators seem happy to discuss their priorities. But managers of a business cannot put any conception of the public good ahead of their private goals: namely, capturing market share and selling advertising, preferably to affluent customers.

David Chiu refers to users of GrassRoots.com as "consumers," not as citizens. He says that he has been told by venture capitalist investors, "if you attract visitors, that is all we care about." Former representative Tom Downey of SpeakOut.com explains, "We have to make [the information on our site] simple, compelling, and interesting."[27] At some point, there will be conflicts between simplicity and substance, or between popularity and seriousness. If commercial sites dominate, substance and seriousness will be hard to find.

Conclusion

It seems, in short, that we need deliberate reform efforts to make the World Wide Web serve public purposes during campaigns. Candidate sites will have limited value until real-world reforms change the incentives that motivate politicians. And independent web sites, although useful, need philanthropic support if they are to survive in a rapidly commercializing cyberspace.

Notes

1. Keith Perine, "Power to the (Web Enabled) People," *The Standard*, 3 April 2000, www.thestandard.com.

2. Elaine Ciulla Kamarck, "Campaigning on the Internet in the Elections of 1998," in *Democracy.com? Governance in a Networked World,* ed. by Elaine Ciulla Kamarck and Joseph S. Nye, Jr., (Hollis, N.H.: Hollis, 1999), 99–123. I am also grateful to Ryan Thornburg of the Democracy Online Project for sending me eleven web sites that were originally collected and saved by the Civic Resource Group.

3. Elizabeth Arnold, "Campaigning on the 'Net,'" *Morning Edition,* National Public Radio, 16 March 1999 (audio copy at www.npr.org/programs/morning/archives/1999/990316.me.html).

4. This is the standard view, endorsed by Curtis Gans of the Committee on the Study of the American Electorate and widely reported in the press. But methods of counting eligible citizens are problematic. See Peter Bruce, "How the Experts Got Voter Turnout Wrong Last Year," *The Public Perspective,* October/November 1997, 39–43. According to Bruce, the year 1988 set the record for lowest turnout in a presidential election.

5. Richard L. Berke, "Democrats' Gains Dispel Notion that the G.O.P. Benefits from Low Turnout," *The New York Times,* 6 November 1998, A28.

6. Steven Rosenstone and John Mark Hansen, *Mobilization, Participation, and Democracy in America* (New York: Macmillan, 1993), 215.

7. Sidney Verba, Kay Lehman Schlozman, and Henry E. Brady, *Voice and Equality: Civic Voluntarism in American Politics* (Cambridge, Mass.: Harvard University Press, 1995), 135, 150.

8. For a good discussion of this thesis, see Pippa Norris, "Who Surfs? New Technology, Old Voters, and Virtual Democracy in the 1996 and 1998 U.S. Elections," in Kamarck and Nye, *democracy.com?,* 71–94.

9. Pew Center for the People and the Press, *The Internet News Audience Goes Ordinary,* press release, 14 January 1999, 80.

10. Kamarck, tables 9 and 11 (pp. 115 and 117).

11. Testimony of Lynn Reed and Max Fose to the Democracy Online Project's National Task Force, 17 April 2000. In 1998, according to the Pew poll, downloading election information and getting information about where to vote together accounted for 32 percent of political Internet use. Other uses, such as sending or receiving e-mail about candidates (22 percent) and getting information about voting records (30 percent), could also have mobilizing effects. However, most of this activity did not occur on web sites created by campaigns. See Pew, *Internet News Audience Goes Ordinary,* 76.

12. According to Kamarck, *"Campaigning on the Internet"*(table 9), 53 percent of the 1998 campaign sites solicited campaign contributions.

13. John Dewey, *The Public and Its Problems* (New York: Henry Holt, 1927), 206–207.

14. The Gore campaign also conducted a few "real-time interactive Town Hall meetings" to "discuss how we can build a better America in the twenty-first century." On these occasions, I presume that the questions were not screened or

prompted. However, as the real-time sessions were not saved, only live participants could view any awkward exchanges that might arise.

15. Public comments at the Democracy Online Project's National Task Force hearings, 17 April 2000.

16. W. Russell Neuman, *Campaign 2000: Web Electioneering Tests the Waters*, at www.netelection.org/commentary/2000003.php3.

17. Testimony of Max Fose to Democracy Online Project's National Task Force, 17 April 2000.

18. Kamarck, "Campaigning on the Internet," 103.

19. Federal Election Commission filings through 20 March 2000, at www.fecinfo.com/fecinfo/.

20. Note, however, that in 1995, 85 percent of all "threads" in USENET political discussions provided "information without a debate." See Kevin A. Hill and John E. Hughes, "Computer-Mediated Political Communications: The USENET and Political Communities," *Political Communication* 14, no. 3 (1997), 16.

21. I defend these reform proposals in *The New Progressive Era: Toward a Fair and Deliberative Democracy* (Lanham, Md.: Rowman & Littlefield, 2000). See also "Consultants and American Political Culture," *Report from the Institute for Philosophy and Public Policy*, summer/fall issue, 1994; "Public Journalism and Deliberation," *Report from the Institute for Philosophy and Public Policy*, winter, 1994; "Expert Analysis vs. Public Opinion: The Case of Campaign Finance Reform," *The Report from the Institute for Philosophy and Public Policy*, summer, 1997.

22. Dennis Thompson, "James Madison on Cyberdemocracy," in Kamarck and Nye, *democracy.com?* 39.

23. GoTo charges customers to be listed prominently. Yahoo! has a "Business Express" www.fecinfo.com/fecinfo/service that costs $199 and "guarantees that within seven days a member of Yahoo!'s editorial staff will look at your site and consider it for inclusion in the Yahoo! directory." Ask Jeeves has signed up "merchant partners" that "may receive preferential placement for payment."

24. Netelection.org video presented at the National Press Club (27 January 2000) of edited interviews with volunteer subjects (produced January 2000).

25. Chiu spoke at the Democracy Online Project's National Task Force hearings, 17 April 2000. See also Declan McCullagh, "Grassroots Site under Fire," *Wired News* (11 April 2000) at www.wired.com. (Editor's note: DNet later became a project of the League of Women Voters.)

26. Public comments at the Democracy Online Project's National Task Force hearings, 17 April 2000.

27. Public comments at National Task Force hearings, 17 April 2000. (Editor's note: By the end of 2000, both GrassRoots and SpeakOut had altered their businesses to de-emphasize voter education and deliberation. GrassRoots focused on the development of software for advocacy groups, and SpeakOut concentrated on message testing.)

Election Law and the Internet   5

TREVOR POTTER AND KIRK L. JOWERS

U.S. Government Regulation of the Internet: The Rule and the Exception

TO DATE, THE United States government has generally allowed the Internet to develop with little or no regulatory intervention. The president and the Congress have both promoted a strong national policy of fostering the continued growth of the Internet and refraining from government regulation. The 1996 Telecommunications Act stated:

> It is the policy of the United States (1) to promote the continued development of the Internet and other interactive computer services and other interactive media; [and] (2) to preserve the vibrant and competitive free market that presently exists for the Internet and other interactive computer services, *unfettered by Federal or State regulation.*[emphasis added][1]

In providing rationales for this hands-off policy, the Act noted that:

1. The rapidly developing array of Internet and other interactive computer services available to individual Americans represent an extraordinary advance in the availability of educational and informational resources to our citizens. . . .
2. The Internet and other interactive computer services offer a forum for a true diversity of political discourse, unique opportunities for cultural development, and myriad avenues for intellectual activity. . . .
3. The Internet and other interactive computer services have flourished, to the benefit of all Americans, *with a minimum of government regulation.*[emphasis added][2]

Most regulatory agencies have followed Congress's lead when considering regulations pertaining to the Internet. For example, the Federal Communications Commission (FCC), in a 1999 report on broadband Internet access, concluded that "[t]he Commission should forbear from imposing regulations and resist the urge to regulate prematurely."[3] The reason? "The Internet, from its roots a quarter century ago as a military and academic research tool, has become a global resource for millions of people. As it continues to grow, the Internet will generate tremendous benefits for the economy and society."[4]

The courts have likewise agreed that keeping "government interference in the medium to a minimum" is necessary to "maintain the robust nature of the Internet communications."[5] In *Reno v. ACLU*,[6] the United States Supreme Court confirmed that Internet communications deserve a high level of First Amendment protection by invalidating portions of the Communications Decency Act. In determining that these provisions were unconstitutional, the Court held that the Internet deserved *more* First Amendment protection than television or radio communications.[7] It stated that justifications for regulation of speech in broadcast media, including its history of extensive government regulation, scarcity, and invasive nature, "are not present in cyberspace."[8] The Court also noted that "the vast democratic fora of the Internet" have not been subject to the type of government regulation that has attended the broadcast industry.[9] (See chapter 6 for the politics behind this 1997 decision.)

To every generalization, however, there is an exception. In contrast to other federal agencies, the Federal Election Commission (FEC) has taken a more activist approach toward the Internet. This happened, in large part, because political activists solicited rulings from the FEC. Almost every politically active individual, group, political action committee (PAC), trade association, corporation, and union moved online during the late 1990s, to both provide and receive everything from messages to money. And they needed clarifications on how ensuing election laws pertained to online campaigning.

Extending federal election law to the Internet raises myriad questions. Most center on whether a candidate or political party is receiving something of value from a contributor via the Internet—and if so, how it is to be valued, when it must be reported, and what responsibilities the receipt imposes on the candidate or party. As described in more detail below, federal election law sets limits on the amount of money individuals and PACs may contribute to federal campaigns, and determines whether contributions or expenditures made by these groups must be reported to the FEC. The law also prohibits contributions and expenditures for the purpose of influencing a federal election by corporations, foreign nationals, and government contractors. A "contribution" is defined as the provision of "anything of value" to a federal candidate or committee, and an "expenditure" is considered a payment made for influencing a federal election. The difficulty lies in determining how exactly these definitions apply to such Internet-related goods as links, operating programs, and messages.

In 1999, the FEC solicited advice from the general public and issued a Notice of Inquiry (NOI): Should the agency establish a set of regulations regarding the Internet and campaigns for federal office, and if so, what should those regulations entail? (For a discussion of one effort to generate a grassroots response to the NOI, see chapter 6.) In 2001, the FEC issued a Notice of Proposed Rulemaking on political use of the Internet, on which it has taken comments and scheduled a public hearing for March 2002. Until such a set of regulations is enacted, campaigning on the Internet will continue to be governed by the patchwork of an ever-evolving set of Advisory Opinions that are periodically issued by the FEC. From the opinions issued to date, some governing principles can be discerned. FEC Advisory Opinions are available on line at www.fec.gov, and an analysis of them may be found at the Brookings Institution's web site, www.brookings .edu/campaignfinance.

FEC Regulation of Online Campaigning

Federal election law operates on the presumption that: 1) communications to the general public about federal candidates cost a lot of money, and 2) campaign spending may be prohibited, limited, and/ or required to be reported in order to curtail financial corruption of the electoral process. When Congress enacted this legislation in the 1970s, the only notable alternative to campaigning consisted merely of standing on a street corner and shouting. That remains one of the few forms of public communication not regulated or reportable under the federal election laws (although it is subject to other laws).

The rise of the Internet as a political medium calls presumption 1 into question. Individuals can reach hundreds of people with listservs and broadcast e-mails. Organizations can mobilize thousands through a posting on a web site. For-profit and nonprofit organizations have sprung up to convey political news on the Internet, complete with links to candidate and party web sites, reprints of candidate materials, interviews and debates with candidates, and polling information. Accessing this network of campaign information and forwarding excerpts from it costs any Internet user practically nothing. Indeed, now that some online service providers make web site creation software available to subscribers as part of their regular service packages, web pages can be created without any identifiable incremental costs. Yet without a cost for communication, current law has nothing to measure, and regulators have no way to monitor the political use of the Internet to find possible financial corruption. The bans on corporate and labor spending for speech on behalf of federal candidates and the limits on in-kind contributions (e.g., donating equipment and professional services) by individuals become difficult to interpret in the Internet context. In interpreting laws, the FEC has previously depended on discrete and identifiable costs for the purchase of advertising to reach the general public; it has presumed that contributions to presidential candidates are only made by check, with signatures in ink on paper.

A greater problem for the FEC is that, prior to the Internet, political speakers were largely parties, candidates, and well-organized groups of persons, all at least passingly familiar with the federal election laws and FEC reporting obligations. Internet political speakers, by contrast, tend to include many individuals who are completely unaware that federal election law may apply to their activity. Internet speakers also include small newsletter publishers and news-based web sites and private nonprofit entities or governmental agencies, all of which assume that the journalistic and/or nonpartisan nature of their activities exempts them from FEC requirements, as it has for their offline counterparts.

The FEC's initial approach was to declare that speech on the Internet does have a cost and must be considered and quantified as something of value to a federal candidate. Logically, that led to the argument that the creation or use of web sites and pages for disseminating federal election-related speech, including news, commentary, and candidate information, should be subject to regulation under the Federal Election Campaign Act of 1971, as amended (FECA). Likewise, providing a link to a federal candidate's web site would be subject to the federal election laws.

More recently, in a trio of 1999 Advisory Opinions issued to the Minnesota secretary of state, the nonprofit entity Democracy Net, and the for-profit Election Zone, the FEC concluded that nonpartisan activity on the Web—loosely defined as providing campaign-related information and candidates' statements in a way that treats all candidates on an equal basis—is exempt from any FEC reporting requirements.[10] In another Advisory Opinion that year, issued to the Bush campaign, the FEC found that Internet activity by campaign volunteers acting on their own need not be tracked and reported by the candidate's campaign committee.[11] These new Advisory Opinions reflect a growing consensus at the FEC that Internet activity should not be burdened by traditional campaign finance regulation unless it involves the expenditure of large sums of money for overtly partisan political speech.

Individual Use of the Internet

Still, any individual who participates in political activities on the Internet must be wary of legal requirements and pitfalls. For example, an individual may spend an unlimited amount of money creating a web site that discusses issues, legislation, and policy—provided that the site does not expressly advocate the election or defeat of a federal candidate. Alternately, an individual may create a web site expressly advocating the election or defeat of a candidate, so long as its construction and maintenance are not coordinated with a federal candidate or the candidate's campaign committee. The costs of creating and maintaining such an independent web site are considered "expenditures," which trigger reporting requirements to the FEC if they exceed $250.[12] For an individual who does coordinate a political web site with a federal campaign committee, the costs are considered in-kind contributions and are counted against his or her annual contribution limit of $1,000 per candidate per election.[13]

What about signing political e-mail and instant messages on behalf of a campaign? If an individual is working as a volunteer for a political campaign, but the campaign does not control the specific volunteer activity, then the personal cost accrued by an individual using the Internet for campaign activity is not considered a contribution to the campaign. As such, these costs would not be counted against an individual's $1,000 contribution limit. A volunteer who is a corporate employee may also use corporate equipment to conduct campaign activity, provided such use is occasional, isolated, and incidental. Otherwise, the campaign must reimburse the costs of the campaign activity to the corporation.[14] Finally, a volunteer who republishes speeches and issue papers by a candidate from the volunteer's home computer may do so without such republication being considered a contribution to the candidate's campaign.[15]

Corporate and Union Use of the Internet

Because federal election law prohibits contributions from corporations and labor unions, neither entity can provide free Internet services to a campaign if these are normally provided for a fee.[16] Likewise, a corporation may not post its candidate endorsements on its supporting PAC web site unless access to the endorsements is confined to members of the corporation's restricted class.[17] A PAC may, however, post a general description of the corporate PAC and information about how to find out more regarding the PAC on web site locations for viewing by employees in or outside the restricted class, provided there are no PAC solicitations posted.

The publication of campaign material on the Internet by a corporation that is a news entity engaged in carrying out a legitimate press function is not considered a contribution, and therefore would not be prohibited under federal election law.[18] This exemption does not apply to nonnews entity corporations.[19] Corporations engaged in the business of assisting political campaigns and PACs in fundraising over the Internet may do so, provided that certain safeguards, such as payment at the usual and ordinary rate, are met.[20]

Political Action Committees

Publicly available information about particular public officials may be posted on PAC web sites without triggering expenditure requirements beyond those already associated with the operation of PACs. Further, nonconnected (independent) PACs (but not corporate PACs) may solicit contributions from the general public through a web site.[21] Nonconnected PACs may post political speeches that expressly advocate the election or defeat of a specific candidate and need only report the costs of doing so as overhead or operating expenses. Examples of these costs are expenses for registering and maintaining a domain name and web site hosting, and any costs relating to the purchase and use of computer hardware and software. These expenses, however, must be reported as independent expenditures if they can be isolated and found to be directly attributable to a clearly identified candidate.[22]

Corporate PACs may engage in such general political speech as well, but must pay for it out of contributed funds only. A PAC sending e-mail that expressly advocates the election or defeat of a clearly identified candidate is engaged in independent expenditure activities that must be reported if the costs exceed $200.[23] Likewise, if 100 or more e-mails containing express advocacy are sent by a PAC, the e-mail must also contain a disclaimer that includes the sponsor's full name and that states whether the e-mail was authorized by a particular candidate.[24]

PACs may receive contributions via electronic employee payroll deductions, provided their employees can electronically revoke or modify their deductions and that the employer keeps records of the transactions.[25] A corporate or trade association PAC may also solicit its restricted class through a PAC web site, but it must ensure—by the use of a password or other security plan—that persons outside the restricted class do not have access to the solicitation.[26]

Fundraising on the Internet by Federal Candidates

Individuals may contribute to political campaigns on the Internet by credit card or electronic check if the campaigns receiving the contributions have appropriate safeguards in place.[27] For presidential candidacies, such contributions are eligible for federal matching funds.[28]

When soliciting contributions, federal candidate committees must include certain disclaimers (e.g., "Paid for by," "not tax deductible," and "no foreign contributions permitted") and also are obligated to use their "best efforts" to obtain the name, address, occupation, and employer of each person who contributes more than $200 during a calendar year.[29] The Commission has determined that a committee making a solicitation "may substitute e-mail communications for written or oral communications as a means of exerting best efforts to obtain missing contributor information where the original contribution was received through the Internet, or where the committee has otherwise obtained reliable information as to the donor's e-mail address."[30]

Candidates should note that federal law requires campaign materials—whether printed or broadcast—that expressly advocate the election or defeat of a federal candidate to contain a disclosure statement that makes clear who paid for the ad.[31] Thus, candidate-sponsored web sites should also bear a disclosure statement stating that they are paid for by the candidate's committee.

The FEC's Internet Rule Making

In November of 1999, the FEC issued an NOI seeking public comment on a wide array of Internet-related campaign and election issues and received more than 1,300 comments from the general public, interest groups, political parties, law firms, labor organizations, Internet companies, and a major Internet service provider.[32] The FEC legal staff then worked from these comments to put together proposed regulations. A Notice of Proposed Rule Making (NPRM) was approved by the Commission in September 2001 and published in the Federal Register with a sixty-day comment period.[33]

The NPRM sought comments on proposed rules addressing three main issues: (1) whether the FEC's "volunteer exemption" is applicable to individuals using personally owned "computer equipment, software, Internet services, or Internet domain name(s) . . . to engage in Internet activity for the purpose of influencing any election to Federal office," so that a contribution or expenditure would not result; (2) whether corporations and labor organizations may establish a hyperlink from their web sites to the web site of a candidate or party committee without a contribution or expenditure resulting; and (3) whether corporations and labor organizations may make candidate endorsements available to the general public on their web sites. The FEC accepted comments on this NPRM through December 3, 2001, and has scheduled a public hearing on issues raised by the NPRM for March 20, 2002. Once the hearing is complete, the FEC will publish its decisions in this rule making on its website, www.fec.gov.

Non-Election Law Issues of the Political Internet

Cybersquatting

In 2000, Congress commissioned the Department of Commerce to study the issue of "cybersquatting"—the registering of Internet domain names containing trademarks or personal names by someone other than the owner of the marks or the person with that name.[34] A domain name, such as yahoo.com or ebay.com, is the address that identifies a particular web site.[35] Such names are issued on a first-come, first-served basis, and name registration requires only a modest investment of less than $100.[36] After completion of the study, the Department recommended that no action be taken.[37]

Realizing that desirable domain names are scarce, cybersquatters have hastened to acquire as many names as they can, including the names of political candidates.[38] Cybersquatters are motivated by a variety of considerations. Some register a politician's name or variation of a name hoping to attract more viewers to their web sites, many of which are parodies of the web sites of actual candidates.[39] Others hold the domain name "hostage" until the candidate agrees to pay a ransom in exchange for the name.[40] Regardless of their motives, cybersquatters create a great deal of confusion among those who want to learn more about the candidates and their positions on the issues, because cybersquatters increase the cost and effort involved in searching for such information.

As search costs rise, so does the likelihood that online citizens will quit their searches before reaching reliable information provided by a particular candidate. Furthermore, a cybersquatter's control over a domain name that is similar to a candidate's name will diminish that candidate's ability to distribute his or her message, because the cybersquatter's site will draw away Internet traffic that was intended for the candidate's official site. Also, the potential for abuse is significant. For example, on at least one occasion, an impostor web site designed to look like that of a particular presidential candidate has taken campaign contributions intended for that candidate.[41] Accordingly, electronic democracy will struggle as a truly transformative force in our political culture until the problems associated with cybersquatting are adequately resolved.

Some potential solutions to the cybersquatting problem include: the FEC creating a web site that includes a registry of hypertext links to each federal candidate's web page; the FEC establishing a site that would serve as a common host for the official web sites of all federal candidates; Congress creating a federal right of publicity for political candidates; or the creation of a new top-level domain (e.g., ".pol") that could be used only by registered candidates.

Copyright and Trademark Law

Despite the fact that the U.S. government thus far has taken a hands-off approach to Internet regulation, operators of political web sites must remain aware that principles of copyright and trademark law still apply in the online environment. In a recent case involving alleged copyright infringement by an Internet company, a federal judge stated that "some companies operating in the area of the Internet may have a misconception that, because their technology is somewhat novel, they are somehow immune from the ordinary applications of the laws of the United States, including copyright law. They need to understand that the law's domain knows no such limits."[42]

The copyright issues raised by the operation of a political web site are similar to those raised by the publication of a newsletter. For instance, a publisher of a newsletter must receive permission before using copyrighted photographs; so must an operator of a web site. Furthermore, both newsletters and web sites must receive authorization before reprinting (in whole or in large part) the writings of others, especially if such reprinting does not include any accompanying commentary. Newsletters and web sites differ in an important respect, however; copyright infringement on the Internet can result in much higher damages than copyright infringement in the newsletter context, primarily because the Internet allows for wider distribution.

Trademark issues also arise when one creates a political web site. Logos, graphics, and slogans used by a campaign are eligible for protection under trademark laws because they identify a particular source or provider of goods or services. Thus, if the operator of a political web site were to copy and use graphics or logos from a campaign site, that operator may be liable for trademark infringement unless he first obtains permission from the campaign.

FCC's Role in Regulating Internet Political Activity

The FCC has an enduring policy of promoting the development of the Internet through forbearance from regulation. Beginning in 1966, in the pre-Internet period, with *In the Matter of Regulatory and Policy Problems Presented by the Interdependence of Computer and Communications Services and Facilities*,[43] and continuing with *In the Matter of*

Federal-State Joint Board on Universal Service (1998),[44] the FCC has refrained from issuing regulations governing the Internet; it has not held the Internet community to the same requirements to which it holds broadcast stations and cable systems.

Specifically, the Communications Act[45] and the FCC's rules require, with several exceptions, broadcast stations and cable systems to provide equal opportunities to opposing legally qualified candidates. The Communications Act and FCC rules also require that during the forty-five days before a primary election and the sixty days before a general election, a station must offer time to political candidates at no more than the rate charged its most favored commercial advertiser for that amount of time and for that class of advertising (such as preemptible or non-preemptible advertising time).[46] The FCC has not attempted to apply these laws and regulations to the Internet.

Conclusion

As this book went to press, the Senate had passed the McCain-Feingold bill, the House had passed the Shays-Meehan bill, and reform leaders in the Senate were planning to attempt to seek a Senate vote to approve the House bill and send it to the president for signature without going to conference. The bills are nearly identical and include significant changes in federal election law. They do not, however, address the Internet regulatory issues that are the subject of this chapter. For all the changes it encompassed, the Internet was only marginally involved: the bill directs the FEC to develop and provide free software, so that campaigns with receipts of $50,000 or more could readily comply with disclosure requirements and the agency could post such data online no later than 48 hours after receiving it. This minimal regulation is in keeping with the approach described in this chapter.

Notes

The authors express their appreciation to attorney Matthew S. Petersen of Wiley, Rein, & Fielding for his significant research, writing, and editorial assistance with this chapter.

1. Telecommunications Act of 1996, Public Law 104–104, 110 Stat. 56, codified at 47 USC § 230(b); see also Telecommunications Act of 1996 § 706

(directing FCC to remove regulatory barriers that discourage the development of advanced telecommunications capability, including Internet access); see generally Digital Tornado: The Internet and Telecommunications Policy, OPP Working Paper Series, ii (March 1997) ("In passing the 1996 Act, Congress expressed its intent to implement a 'procompetitive deregulatory national communications policy'").

2. PL 104–104, 47 USC § 230(a).

3. Federal Communications Commission, Broadband Today (Oct. 1999) at 41. Available online at //ftp.fcc.gov/Bureaus/Cable/Reports/broadbandtoday .pdf.

4. Digital Tornado at i.

5. Zeran v. America Online, Inc., 129 F3d 327, 330 (4th Cir. 1997).

6. 521 US 844 (1997).

7. at 868.

8. at 868.

9. at 868–69.

10. Federal Election Commission (FEC) Advisory Opinion 2000–7 (Alcatel); see also FEC Advisory Op. 2000–10 (COMPAC).

11. 11CFR § 110.11(a).

12. FEC Advisory Op. 1998–22 (Smith).

13. FEC, Smith.

14. FEC Advisory Op. 1999–17 (Bush).

15. FEC, Bush.

16. FEC Advisory Op. 1999–22 (Aristotle Publishing).

17. FEC Advisory Op. 1997–16 (Oregon Natural Resources Council Action Federal PAC).

18. FEC Advisory Op. 1996–16 (Bloomberg); see also FEC Advisory Op. 2000–13 (iNEXTV).

19. FEC Advisory Op. 1996–2 (CompuServe).

20. FEC Advisory Op. 1999–22 (Aristotle Publishing).

21. FEC Advisory Op. 1995–9 (NewtWatch).

22. FEC Advisory Op. 1999–37 (X-PAC); see also FEC Advisory Op. 1997–16 (ONRCAF PAC).

23. FEC Advisory Op. 1999–37 (X-PAC).

24. FEC, X-PAC.

25. FEC Advisory Op. 1999–3 (Microsoft).

26. FEC Advisory Op. 2000–10 (COMPAC).

27. FEC Advisory Op. 1999–9 (Bill Bradley for President, Inc.); FEC Advisory Op. 1999–36 (Campaign Advantage).

28. 11 CFR §§ 9034.2 & 9034.3; see FEC Advisory Op. 1999–36 (Campaign Advantage).

29. 11 CFR § 104.7(b).

30. FEC Advisory Op. 1999–17 (Bush).

31. 11 CFR § 110.11(a)(1).

32. Use of the Internet for Campaign Activity, 64 Fed. Reg. 60360 (proposed Nov. 5, 1999), to be codified at 11 CFR pts. 100, 102, 103, 104, 106, 107, 109, 114, and 116. See www.fec.gov/register.htm; see also www.brookings.edu/dybdocroot/gs/cf/sourcebk01/InternetChap.pdf (Potter and Jowers article on FEC Internet regulation).

33. The Internet and Federal Elections; Candidate-Related Materials on Web Sites of Individuals, Corporations, and Labor Organizations, 66 Fed. Reg. 50358 (proposed Oct. 3, 2001), to be codified at 11 CFR pts. 100, 114, and 117.

34. PL 106–113, 113 Stat. 1501.

35. Richard Lehv, "Cybersquatting in Focus: Are New Rules Needed or Will Existing Laws Suffice?" *N.Y.L.J.*, 18 Jan. 2000, at S4.

36. Richard J. Grabowski, "Strategies for Securing and Protecting Your Firm's Domain Name," *Legal Tech Newsl.*, Feb. 2000, at 7.

37. Department of Commerce, Report to Congress: The Anticybersquatting Consumer Protection Act of 1999, section 3006 concerning the abusive registration of domain names, www.uspto.gov/web/offices/dcom/olia/tmcybpiracy/repcongress.pdf.

38. Grabowski, supra note 3, at 7.

39. Robert D. Gilbert, "Squatters Beware: There Are Two New Ways to Get You," *N.Y.L.J.*, 24 Jan. 2000, at T5; see Phyllis Plitch, "Bounty Hunter, New Law Put Squeeze on Net Domain-Name Cybersquatters," *Wall St. J.*, 20 Dec. 1999, available on Westlaw in 1999 WL-WSJ 24926545.

40. Gilbert, "Squatters Beware."

41. Brian Blomquist and Daniel Jeffreys, "FBI Crashes Campaign Web-Scam Site," *N.Y. Post*, 20 February 2000, at 26.

42. UMG Recordings, Inc. v. MP3.com, Inc., 2000, available on Westlaw, WL 1262528, at *6 (S.D.N.Y. 2000).

43. 7 FCC 2d 11 (1966).

44. Report to Congress, 13 FCC Rcd 8776 (1998).

45. *Communications Act of 1934*, as amended.

46. For example, if a station normally charges $100 for a particular advertisement but sells it for $90 to a commercial advertiser that purchases 100 ads, the candidate is also charged $90, even if he purchases only one ad. To receive the lowest unit charge, the advertising must contain either the candidate's voice or photo likeness, and the candidate's appearance must be in connection with his or her campaign. The lowest unit charge is available only to the candidate or his or her representative. During times outside of the forty-five-day and sixty-day periods, stations must charge political candidates rates that are comparable to those charged to commercial advertisers.

Digital Grass Roots: Issue Advocacy in the Age of the Internet

6

JERRY BERMAN AND DEIRDRE K. MULLIGAN

D EMOCRACY IS REALIZED not only in the voting booth, but also in the manifold forms of interaction in which citizens individually and collectively seek to influence the actions of institutions, both governmental and corporate. The United States has a rich tradition of interest group advocacy, but the barriers to effective communication among individuals, organizations, the media, and policy makers have often been high. The unique qualities of the Internet—its being inexpensive, decentralized, user-controlled—hold the potential not only to revitalize the electoral process, but also to enhance democratic participation in issue advocacy in ways that empower individuals and nonprofit organizations. On legislative, regulatory, and policy issues at the local, state, and federal levels as well as in campaigns directed at corporations, the Internet offers new, inexpensive, interactive, and rapid opportunities for citizens to make their voices heard.

The Unique Architecture and Economics of the Internet

The Internet is a unique medium, distinct from broadcast, print, and cable. As the Supreme Court found in its landmark 1997 decision in *Reno v. ACLU*, the Internet constitutes a "new marketplace of ideas."[1] The Internet affords individual citizens a platform previously available only to the print and broadcast gatekeepers and to those who could afford to purchase air time or space in a newspaper. The economics of the Internet allow any individual to be a broadcaster and a publisher: "Through the use of chat rooms, any person with a phone line can become a town crier with a voice that resonates farther than it could from any soapbox. Through the use of web pages, mail exploders, and newsgroups, the same individual can become a pamphleteer."[2]

Several features of the Internet are supportive of online advocacy. The Internet is:

- Decentralized and open. Traditional mass media are based on systems of limited distribution channels controlled by a relatively small number of entities, or gatekeepers. In contrast, the Internet is decentralized, open, and distributed. It is a network of networks consciously designed to function without gatekeepers.
- Global. The Internet provides immediate access to information from around the world. With simple e-mail, it is as easy and inexpensive to send a message to another continent as to the building across the street. Search engines on the World Wide Web list local and international sites without distinction. Those wishing to avoid government regulation can quickly "mirror" content on servers outside the reach of censors.
- Abundant and inexpensive. The architecture of mass media creates scarcity, but the Internet's architecture places little limit on the amount and diversity of information that can be made available. As the Supreme Court stated in *Reno v. ACLU*, "Unlike the conditions that prevailed when Congress first authorized regulation of the broadcast spectrum, the Internet can hardly be considered a scarce expressive commodity. It provides relatively unlimited, low-cost capacity for communication of all kinds."[3]
- Interactive and user-controlled. Unlike the one-way transmissions typical of radio and television, the Internet is bidirectional: Individuals can speak as well as listen. Unlike television and radio, the Internet is a user-controlled medium. As the Supreme Court found, individuals are not assaulted by information on the Internet but rather enjoy an unequalled ability to direct and control the information with which they come in contact.

The Internet's Impact on Issue Advocacy

Because of these unique architectural and economic qualities, the Internet is changing the ways in which advocacy organizations communicate, educate, organize, and mobilize.

In the first instance, the Internet drastically reduces the costs of communicating. Compare the cost of printing a two-page letter and mailing it to an organization's membership with the cost of sending out the same letter via electronic mail. For any organization with a computer and a telephone line, the incremental cost of weekly, even daily mailings, is near zero—even if the membership numbers in the hundreds of thousands. Today, it is common for issue organizations, even those with small staffs and budgets, to issue weekly updates to their members. This allows organizations to maintain a highly informed membership. And e-mail has a multiplier effect: Because a message is easily retransmitted—the recipient bears no additional costs for copying or transmission—e-mail updates can be passed along to colleagues, friends, and family in a virtual chain letter.

E-mail enables organizations to disseminate information rapidly. Time is often a deciding factor in whether individuals who care about an issue can influence the outcome of a debate or the coverage of an issue in the traditional media, and in "Internet time," organizations can quickly and broadly disseminate information as soon as it is received.

Although electronic mailing lists and listservs are the cheapest and possibly still the most effective means of distributing information, organizations are increasingly using their web sites for issue advocacy. Less sophisticated sites serve merely as clearinghouses of information, archiving reports, press releases, and testimony and offering links to relevant legislative and regulatory materials, news articles, and other documents. More sophisticated web sites include features that prompt visitors to take specific democratic actions based on the information presented, for example, combining simple talking points with a direc-tory allowing visitors to use their zip codes to find the names and tele-phone numbers of their member of Congress. Some sites then allow users to send an e-mail, fax, or telegram from the web page to their elected representative.

At the Center for Democracy and Technology (COT), we recom-mend that voters make a telephone call. We have found that e-mails and form faxes are often ignored in congressional offices. Indeed, we also have posted the town meeting schedules for members of a key committee, encouraging visitors to our web site to speak to their member of Congress in person, back home in the district, where an informed contact from a constituent can have tremendous impact.

E-mail and the Web have not eliminated the importance of traditional media as message disseminators for advocacy organizations, but they have changed it. Increasingly, articles in the printed versions of newspapers and magazines will include links referring readers to the web sites of organizations quoted in the story. Online editions of television and cable news programs and the web pages of major newspapers are loaded with hyperlinks. A guest on a radio or television show can easily mention the URL of his or her site, and the producers may run the Internet address with a speaker's name on the screen. Ironically, in all these ways, a quote or reference in the traditional press can prove far more valuable than ever before by attracting traffic to the organization's web site—even though the traditional media are no longer critical to ensuring the availability of the message in the first place.

At its most sophisticated, the interactive nature of the Internet allows content on web sites to be tailored according to information provided by visitors. For example, an interactive form can allow a visitor to provide his or her zip code and in return receive information such as the voting records, committee assignments, or policy positions of his or her representative and senators. Similarly, an advocacy organization can customize the content presented to the user upon the user's return visit, depending, for example, on whether he or she was interested in environmental issues affecting Vermont or those affecting California.

The user-controlled nature of the Internet makes it easier for smaller and new organizations that do not have widespread name recognition to reach individuals interested in a given issue. The global nature of the medium ensures that such organizations can be found regardless of geographic and political boundaries. In this, as in other ways, the Internet has had a leveling effect. Although some users rely on menus at major portals and online services, which tend to favor more established organizations, many more users rely on search engines to locate information. (There are serious limitations to current search engine technology, and the process of finding and ranking useful information online remains one of the major challenges facing the Net. See chapter 7 for more on this.) Although a person's starting point onto the Internet is still important, it is likely to have less control than in the past over the content that the individual will ultimately view. The ability of users to jump from site to site lessens the importance of entry points, posing opportunities and risks for advocacy organizations.

At this point, it appears that there is little correlation between one's monetary resources and one's effectiveness in using the Internet. The Internet rewards flexibility and speed and disfavors hierarchy; larger organizations may therefore find it more difficult to fully utilize the Internet for advocacy. Indeed, the advent of the Internet has encouraged the development of a growing number of issue advocates who operate without an organization or membership per se, devoting only their time and energy to spreading their message.

The Four Levels of Online Advocacy

Major political parties, government organizations, business and trade associations, unions, nonpartisan public interest groups, and individuals have all turned to the Internet to get their message across, influence public opinion, and drive policy. Issues and strategies differ, but online campaigns work at one or more of four levels.

E-Mail That Spreads Like a Virus

Several effective issue advocacy campaigns have been exclusively e-mail driven. E-mail is the simplest means of spreading information. It puts a message directly in front of individuals. It requires no production or graphic skills and little in the way of computer infrastructure and support. Perhaps most importantly, every recipient can simply and quickly forward the e-mail to others. If the message is compelling, then with a little luck an e-mail or online posting can achieve the ultimate in online advocacy: it can propagate throughout the Internet like a virus.

Two campaigns highlight the enormous impact that the removal of economic barriers to message dissemination can have on issue advocacy. In each instance, individuals were prompted by an e-mail to take a specific action to express their dislike for a specific proposal or product. As a result of each of these campaigns, a government agency or corporation changed its position. These campaigns were both leaderless; they are examples of the nearly pure grassroots, citizen-driven response that the Internet fosters.

- Case Study: Lexis-Nexis P-Trak

   In June 1996, Lexis-Nexis, a searchable online legal and news archive, released P-Trak, a database containing personal information from one of the major credit bureaus. The database provided access to individuals' current addresses, previous addresses, and other personal information. When first announced, the database also included social security numbers, the key that could unlock many other databases of personal information. P-Trak was marketed to the legal community for assistance in locating witnesses, heirs, litigants, and shareholders, but anyone willing to pay the monthly fee could subscribe.

Soon, a message was posted to a newsgroup detailing the service and the information available. The message, of unknown origin, stated: "Your name, social security number, current address, previous addresses, mother's maiden name, birth date and other personal information are now available to anyone with a credit card through a new Lexis database called P-Trak." The message went on to urge people to call Lexis-Nexis and remove their names from the database.[4] That message was taken and passed from newsgroup to newsgroup, listserv to listserv. Tens of thousands of Internet users are estimated to have received at least one copy of the chain-letter e-mail, which a Lexis-Nexis representative described as the "e-mail that wouldn't die." Thousands phoned Lexis-Nexis, which hired additional operators to handle the increase in calls. The traditional print and broadcast media took notice of the speed and pervasiveness with which the e-mail traveled, interpreting it as a sign of public outrage with privacy violations in general, generating further participation in the campaign.

Lexis-Nexis quickly decided to remove social security numbers from the P-Trak product. Ultimately, the controversy influenced government policy. On September 20, 1996, the Federal Trade Commission (FTC) recommended that Congress amend the Fair Credit Reporting Act to protect the privacy of personal information. Congress directed the Federal Reserve Board to investigate the sale of "sensitive consumer identification information" and whether such sales create "an undue potential for fraud." More broadly, the controversy ignited pressure for regulation of similar "look-up services."

The P-Trak e-mail had spread like a virus as it was passed from one individual to another. The campaign was entirely decentralized. No organization claimed credit for the original message. In fact, efforts to track down the original message and its subsequent path were inconclusive.

- Case Study: Know Your Customer
    In December 1998, federal regulatory agencies responsible for financial institutions proposed a set of Know Your Customer (KYC) regulations for the nation's banks. The proposed rules would have required banks to build profiles on all their customers and report any "suspicious" activity to the federal government's Financial Crimes Enforcement Network, which would in turn enter that information into the Internal Revenue Service's Suspicious Activity Reporting (SAR) System. SAR System data would be shared among several government agencies. The agencies proposing the KYC regulations invited comments on the issue.

    Organizations ranging from the Libertarian Party and the Free Congress Foundation to the American Civil Liberties Union (ACLU) sprang into action over the Internet, alerting their members and urging them to file comments with the regulatory agencies. The e-mail campaign was one component of these organizations' larger efforts, which included talk radio and print and broadcast media, but it was the e-mail campaign that captured the public's attention. Nearly 300,000 negative comments were filed in response to the notice of proposed rule making. Many of the comments were generated from the web site DefendYourPrivacy.com, run by the Libertarian Party. Steve Dasbach, national director of the Libertarian Party, said, "We're hoping to create a chain-letter-type phenomenon, where people visit our web site, file a comment to the FDIC (Federal Deposit Insurance Corporation), and then let more of their friends know about this resource. . . . Basically, we want to put the power of the Internet—and the proprivacy ideology of most cybercitizens—to work to defeat this regulation."[5] That is precisely what happened. In March 1999, the government withdrew its KYC proposal.

Issue Ad-Hocracy

It is widely recognized that the Internet bridges geographic distances. It may be less appreciated how the Internet also bridges political distances, allowing individuals from across traditional ideologies and from many different organizations—individuals who normally would have little contact with each other on matters of activism—to contact each other and collaborate on specific issues. Often these ad-hoc affiliations form around a single action item. At some level, this form of online organizing is more akin to organizing a rally than it is to coalition building in the traditional sense, but in other instances, these ad-hoc groups will mature and evolve into institutions of their own. In either case, the borderless nature of the Internet allows people to come together in previously impossible ways, as shown in these examples:

- ▪ Case Study: The Communications Decency Act

  In 1997, in the landmark *Reno v. ACLU* decision, the Supreme Court unanimously declared unconstitutional the Communications Decency Act (CDA), which had previously made it illegal to post indecent material online in a way that was accessible to minors. The case brought together in opposition to the Act not only civil liberties groups like CDT and the ACLU, but also the American Library Association, corporations such as Time-Warner and America Online (before their merger), and thousands of Internet users and web site operators. The Court's opinion stands as the benchmark for Internet free speech; its factual section includes a brilliant description of the uniquely decentralized, user-controlled architecture of the Internet, qualities that the Court found entitled the Internet to the highest form of First Amendment protection.

  But the path to a unanimous decision upholding free speech online was not foreordained. The CDA was enacted as part of the massive and highly contested Telecommunications Reform Act of 1996. Although civil liberties groups had clearly understood the CDA's serious implications for online freedom of expression and had fought the proposal from the moment of its inception, the Internet and communications industries were reluctant to be seen as defending pornography online and did not mount a strong opposition to the proposal as it moved through Congress. The broader Internet community, dispersed nationwide, libertarian in spirit, and not used to having to pay attention to Washington, was initially unaware of the bill. The process by which the CDA came to be recognized as a censorship law serves as a model of ad-hoc online activism.

As the CDA was nearing passage in Congress, CDT and a tiny group called the Voters Telecommunications Watch (VTW) conceived the Paint the Web Black campaign as a public education device. VTW and CDT began an e-mail campaign urging webmasters to turn the backgrounds on their pages black on the day that President Clinton signed the bill into law. At 11 A.M. on February 8, 1996, the President signed the bill and thousands of web pages went black for forty-eight hours. The effort was more than a statement of outrage. With the participation of high-profile web sites including Netscape, Yahoo!, and RealAudio and with widespread coverage in the traditional media, Paint the Web Black brought the CDA to the attention of many ordinary Internet users and to the broader public. It helped to turn what was once an Internet-only issue tainted by association with pornography into a mainstream fight for civil liberties online.

At the same time, CDT and others organized the Citizens' Internet Empowerment Coalition (CIEC), an ad-hoc coalition of corporations, nonprofit groups, and individual citizens. On February 26, 1996, CIEC filed a lawsuit in federal court in Philadelphia challenging the constitutionality of the CDA. The CIEC lawsuit was combined with one filed earlier by the ACLU. CIEC enlisted thousands of Web publishers to file affidavits in the case, describing the impact that the CDA would have on their freedom of speech. Through a Web-based petition, CIEC signed up more than 115,000 members in five months and also collected funds to support itself. The CIEC web site furnished members and other visitors with information relating to the ongoing lawsuit and general reference links on free speech issues.

The educational and advocacy campaigns initiated by VTW, CDT, and CIEC in opposition to the CDA had a decisive impact on public perception of the policy question posed by the CDA, and they framed the case for the Supreme Court's consideration. Initial reporting on the CDA portrayed the law as an antipornography measure and framed the debate as one about the accessibility of pornography online. The CIEC coalition, however, included the American Library Association, Microsoft, America Online (AOL), and others having little interest in the distribution of pornography; they claimed credibly that the Act would infringe on their free speech, too. The Paint the Web Black campaign visually alerted the public and the media of the potential wide-reaching impact of the law. The focus of reporting in the traditional media shifted from pornography to free speech. The posture of the case before the courts changed: it became a case about the architecture of the Internet.

The breadth of individual citizen participation in the CIEC campaign and in the "Internet blackout" would not have been possible without the Internet. Both efforts were magnified by the thousands of individual citizens who redistributed alerts and built their own informational resource about the CDA based on information from CIEC, CDT, and VTW. Similarly, the Internet enabled the CIEC coalition to solicit and gain unprecedented participation from small publishers and individual citizens in the litigation. Through the Internet, CIEC was able to reach a wide range of Internet publishers in a manner that would have been prohibitively expensive and time-consuming if attempted through other means. By and large, the individuals and small web site publishers who participated in the lawsuit through CIEC had no prior affiliation with CDT or any other CIEC coalition member. The real-time, two-way communication and interaction facilitated by the Internet allowed like-minded citizens and businesses across the country to find one another and participate in a year-long effort to influence public policy.

- Case Study: MoveOn

  MoveOn.org, formed during the 1998 impeachment proceedings of President Clinton, is an example of a grassroots organization initially developed solely on the Internet and around a single moment in history. MoveOn was created by a group of Silicon Valley entrepreneurs in a home office with no funding. In September 1998, they launched a petition site for a Censure and Move On campaign, urging Congress to punish President Clinton by censure, but not to impeach him. Within one week, the campaign had collected 100,000 signatures. In less than twelve weeks, it had signed up 500,000 supporters and received pledges of $13 million. As the impeachment proceedings continued, the campaign expanded to include downloadable banners and posters, e-mail updates, phone campaigns, and physical in-person lobbying.

After the House of Representatives voted for impeachment, the campaign adopted the slogan "We Will Remember": a pledge by the organizers and petitioners to support in the 2000 elections (through volunteer time and money) those who voted against impeachment and to work to defeat those who voted for it. The MoveOn web site accepted donations for specific candidates or for the MoveOn PAC that was formed to administer We Will Remember pledges. On the drive's first day, MoveOn received $5 million pledged for congressional campaigns.[6] And 30,000 people pledged 750,000 hours of volunteer time to defeat proimpeachment legislators. Although the actual totals were smaller than the pledges (a common occurrence), MoveOn compiled an impressive record for the 2000 elections. It made its largest (bundled) donation to Adam Schiff, who unseated impeachment leader James Rogan of California. (Bundling is the gathering of campaign contributions by a person or political organization from numerous individuals and the delivery of the contributions to a specific candidate.)

Becoming Your Own Publisher

Before the Internet, advocacy organizations always feared that no media outlet would cover their actions and policy positions. They would call a press conference and no reporters would come, or they would issue a report and no stories would be written on it. But on the Internet, anyone can be a publisher. The Internet does not eliminate the importance of a front page story in *The New York Times* or a segment on the network news, but the availability of the Web gives every advocacy organization the credible threat that it can make some uncomfortable fact public. Even if a web site is not visited frequently, the mere ability to put a piece of information online can have a powerful impact. In the past, citizens and advocacy organizations had to navigate their way through the gatekeepers of traditional media— reporters, editorial boards, broadcasters—before they could reach the broader public. With the advent of the Internet, citizens and advocacy organizations can speak directly to the public via web sites, e-mail, and other communication vehicles.

▪ Case Study: The Pentium PSN

An example of this power to be one's own publisher arose when the computer chip maker Intel announced that its Pentium III chip would include a Processor Serial Number (PSN): a unique number incorporated into the main chip used in many personal computers. When a personal computer with the Pentium III chip connected to a web site or server or to another computer, this PSN would be transmitted, thus identifying the computer. There was concern that the PSN could be associated not only with a computer, but with an individual user, a particularly disturbing prospect given the Pentium's presence in 75 percent of all personal computers. Opposition to the PSN arose in various forms.

CDT filed a complaint at the Federal Trade Commission asking it to enjoin shipment of Pentium III chips with the PSN "turned on." Aware of the caution with which the FTC was likely to approach such a request, CDT also wrote to the computer manufacturers who used Intel chips in their products. CDT outlined its privacy concerns with the PSN and asked the manufacturers to explain how they intended to respond to the privacy threat posed by the PSN. CDT informed the manufacturers that their answers, or their failure to respond, would be made available to the public and the press through CDT's web site. Within days, all but one of the manufacturers responded, stating that they would take steps to limit the potential privacy impact of the PSN by disabling it prior to shipment or by giving users a ready means of turning it off, thus refuting Intel's claim that introduction of the PSN was in response to customer demands. CDT immediately posted the manufacturers' responses on its web site. This clear, early rejection of the PSN feature by the other manufacturers contributed to the growing sense in the marketplace that the PSN was not a desirable feature. As the privacy controversy continued to swirl, few applications for the PSN were developed and, ultimately, Intel dropped the PSN feature from its next generation of chips. There were many factors in this corporate decision, but as the debate unfolded, CDT's unquestioned ability to "publish" online, even to a tiny audience, any information it received gave it powerful leverage.

Gateways to Participation

Many government processes allow comments from the public. Private corporations too, while not required to, generally accept criticism, praise, and suggestions from the public. However, individuals often find communicating with the government and businesses frustrating: relevant addresses for directing comments may be hard to find, and the official presentation of issues may be complex and highly technical. For the ordinary citizen, it is hard to identify "actionable moments": ones when there is a decision pending at a stage when public input could actually affect the outcome. Using the power of the Internet, advocacy organizations can create more accessible avenues of public participation, providing citizens with plain language interfaces and simplified templates for letters to Congress, comments to regulatory agencies, and complaints to businesses.

- Case Study: The Federal Election Commission Inquiry

In many cases, federal agencies, before adopting regulations, must provide the public with notice and the ability to comment. Generally, these notices are printed in the *Federal Register*, a daily newsprint and online publication of small type and bureaucratic prose that the general public rarely sees or takes note of. Many federal agencies also post proposed regulations on their web sites and, with growing frequency, agencies accept e-mail or Web-based comments from the public. But the highly technical or legalistic language of many such notices remains beyond the understanding of most citizens. Advocacy organizations can use the Internet to mediate between the government and citizens, distilling the complex notices and creating easy formats for comments.

In 1999, the Federal Election Commission issued a notice of inquiry on the extent to which election-related activity on the Internet should be regulated under the campaign finance laws. At issue were important free speech rights of individual citizens. However, the notice was seventeen pages long and written in complex regulatory language. Few individual citizens saw the notice or had the prior expertise to recognize its significance. It looked as though only the political parties and the larger interest groups would respond, through their lawyers.

To lower the hurdle of complexity, CDT created an online resource to make it easier for Web users to understand the issue and file comments in their own words. CDT broke the FEC's complex notice down into nine questions of importance to individual citizens using the Internet. We clarified each question with examples. After each question, we provided a Web-based form that individuals could use to submit their own comments on any or all of the nine questions. When users clicked "Send," their comments would be sent directly to the correct e-mail address at the FEC, formatted with the proper docket number and keyed to the FEC's own outline of the issues.

Within a matter of days, hundreds of individuals used the site to submit comments to the FEC. These were not formulaic comments. "Canned" e-mail comments are devalued the same way that preprinted postcards are; some agencies will count hundreds or thousands of similar comments as just one. Through the use of a Web-based resource, CDT could provide individuals with assistance, and ensure that they spoke in their own voice.

- Case Study: DoubleClick's Merged Profiles

  DoubleClick is a company that places customized advertisements on Web users' browsers based on profiles it compiles of visitors' other online activities. The profiling information is collected through a small identification number or "cookie" that DoubleClick places on a user's hard drive when he or she visits the web site of a DoubleClick client. DoubleClick collects data about visitors from many highly trafficked web sites.

  DoubleClick had always said that the profiles it collected were anonymous—they were linked to a computer, but not to an individual. Thus, privacy alarm bells went off when DoubleClick announced in 1999 that it was merging with Abacus-Direct, a company that specialized in offline direct mail and that held a database containing the names, addresses, and retail purchasing habits of 90 percent of American households. It was apparent that DoubleClick intended to reverse its policy and to merge online surfing habits with offline identity and purchasing records, posing a grave threat to privacy and anonymity.

  CDT began a consumer education and action campaign to alert Internet users to DoubleClick's database merger plan. CDT directed the thousands of activists on its e-mail list to a newly created web site. This site allowed them to protest DoubleClick's action by sending e-mail to DoubleClick and to companies using its ad placement service.

  The CDT web site also told visitors how to opt out of the

DoubleClick profiling system. At the time, DoubleClick allowed consumers to choose not to have information collected about them, but the process of opting out was often cumbersome. Even if a customer was savvy enough to know that DoubleClick was setting cookies, it was hard to find where on DoubleClick's web site the opt-out option was offered. CDT created a set of online forms to assist individuals in opting out of DoubleClick's profiling, as well as other companies' data collection and use practices, on the theory that more individuals would opt out of DoubleClick's profiling if they had the information about how to do it.

In a matter of weeks, tens of thousands of individuals used CDT's resource to opt out of the DoubleClick system and other online data collection systems. In addition, thousands of visitors to CDT's web site sent e-mail to DoubleClick's president protesting the data merger plan. Others e-mailed various companies in the DoubleClick network expressing concern with the plan and asking what personal information was being collected from their sites by DoubleClick. The e-mail campaign was combined with other actions, including a complaint to the Federal Trade Commission (FTC) asking it to block DoubleClick's plan. In the face of public criticism, queries from its busines partners, and intense media scrutiny, DoubleClick put its plan on hold and, in the summer of 2000, reached agreement with the FTC to offer consumers clearer choices in preventing both online collection of information and the merging of that information with offline identities.

Conclusion

Democracy is more than elections. It is also lobbying, protests, pamphlets, petitions, meetings, organizing, and educating. It is all the ways in which citizens and consumers make their voices heard to influence decisions. (Also see chapter 2.) Democracy is communicating to persuade. For these aspects of democracy, the Internet is a powerful new tool for activism. It places in the hands of any individual with a computer and a phone line a previously unimaginable amount of information about government and institutional processes, and it allows that same individual to speak out—to be his or her own publisher—and to identify, communicate with, and join others who share a similar viewpoint.

The Internet does not supplant the traditional components of democracy, including interest groups and the traditional media. To the contrary, the Internet heightens their importance, for citizens still need guidance through the expanded maze of information available to them. The most effective online advocacy campaigns are those that not only empower individuals, but also mediate between them and the government, involving ordinary citizens in the policy process by facilitating prompt, informed communications. Effective online campaigns interact with broadcast and print media, using traditional outlets to drive more traffic to an online action. And effective online advocates recognize that there is no electronic substitute for personal interaction: the Internet can notify people of a town meeting and can educate them so they can speak knowledgeably, but the most effective form of lobbying is still one person speaking directly to another person.

Leading up to the Supreme Court's decision in the CDA matter, one of the lower court judges wrote: "The Internet is a far more speech-enhancing medium than print, the village green, or the mails."[7] So long as the Internet remains an open, decentralized medium with no gatekeepers, it will enhance the communication potential of groups and individuals, deepening the practice of democracy.

Notes

1. *Reno v. ACLU,* 521 US 844 (1997). The Supreme Court based its decision on the District Court's detailed findings of fact, which remain perhaps the best statement of the relevant characteristics of the Internet for purposes of First Amendment analysis. The District Court opinion is online at www.ciec.org/decision_PA/decision_text.html. The Supreme Court's opinion is online at www.ciec.org/SC_appeal/decision.shtml.

2. *Reno v. ACLU,* 521 US at 870.

3. *Reno v. ACLU,* 521 US 844, 870 (1997).

4. Laurie J. Flynn, "Lexis-Nexis Flap Prompts Push for Privacy Rights," *The New York Times,* 13 October 1996.

5. Libertarian Party, *LP Launches New Website to Defeat FDIC's Know Your Customer Proposal,* press release, March 1999, www.lp.org/lpn/9903-kyc.html; see also statement of Phyllis Schlafly, *'Know Your Customer' Stirs up a Hornet's Nest,* Eagle Forum, www.eagleforum.org/alert/knowyour-customer/know

your-customer.html; Robert O'Harrow, Jr., "Disputed Bank Plan Dropped; Regulators Bow to Privacy Fears," *Washington Post*, 24 March 1999, E1.

6. "Frequently Asked Questions," www.moveon.org/faq.htm; Jacob Weisberg, *Will Net Politics Explode in 2000?* 24 September 1999, www.cnn.com/ TECH/computing/9909/24/campaign.2000.idg/.

7. *ACLU v. Reno*, 929 F. Supp. 824, 882 (ED Pa. 1996).

CITIZEN PARTICIPATION AND THE INTERNET III

Adding in the Net: Making Citizenship Count in the Digital Age

7

MICHAEL CORNFIELD

The Airplane Stimulus

FOR THE INTERNET to serve democracy, everyday citizens should be able to use it to have a say in official decisions that govern their lives. In 1999, I felt the urge to citizenship every time I heard a plane fly over my house as I sought, via the Internet, to stop a senatorial policy initiative to increase the number of planes that did so. The events of September 11, 2001 severed that mental association of airplane noise and citizenship. But let me tell my story.

I live near Washington National Airport.[1] Before my wife and I took out a mortgage on the house, I parked outside it at different times of the day and listened to the roar of the jets. It wasn't so bad with the car windows rolled up. The greatest noise occurred during rush hour periods. If we could learn to ignore that as ambient sound, it would keep the problem at an acceptable level. Besides, National was one of four airports in the nation with government restrictions on the number of arrivals and departures allowed in a day. A regional transportation plan, administered by the Metropolitan Washington Airports Authority (MWAA), called for expansion of other area airports, but not the one in our neighborhood.

Then, a few months after we moved in, the planes seemed to move in with us and would not leave. I called National and was patched into a preternaturally calm fellow whose job it has been for years to field noise complaints. He explained that unusual weather patterns had led the air traffic controllers to divert planes into little-used approach and takeoff paths that, evidently, ran right over our house. Sure enough, after a few days, the weather changed and the noise retreated to the background.

A few months later, I learned from the *Washington Post* that John McCain, Chairman of the Senate Commerce Committee, was determined to upset the regional transportation plan and the legal restrictions to bring forty-eight more flights per day to National. An earlier McCain attempt to increase the number of flights by twenty-four per day had been rebuffed in the House of Representatives; in demanding forty-eight in his second try, he was perhaps angling for the original twenty-four as a "compromise" outcome. McCain argued that the move would bring the benefits of business competition to the Washington, D.C. air travel market. His opponents noted the existing healthy state of competition among airline companies for slots at Washington-area airports. The newspaper pointed out the financial contributions of Phoenix-based America West Airlines to McCain's campaigns and the fact that the Arizona senator was also calling for an end to the prohibition on long-haul flights to National, which has short and unexpandable runways. McCain did more than advocate. He bottled up funding for regional airport improvements in pursuit of his goals.

I experienced a movie moment of civic outrage. I did not want to move, I could not afford soundproofing, and I resented McCain's special interest trumping the arrangement the democratic process had generated. So I would stand up and speak out. I would join hands with local residents, our elected representatives, and aviation experts and officials. Our coalition would stop McCain from putting his convenience and cronyism ahead of our peace of mind and sense of justice.

I thought the Internet would help me find, consolidate, and motivate this coalition. No senator could bottle up this decentralized network. I saw individuals communicating back and forth at will. A few would summon computer power to ensure that the action plans laid would be the best the data allowed. Then, at the click of a mouse, the coalition would spring to life, showering dollars, talking points, and pledged votes at the next election exactly where they would have optimal impact. Was that too much to expect? I would not know unless I tried.

Getting Smart: Keyword versus Password Intelligence

The emergence of the Internet in society affords individuals new opportunities to participate in democratic politics. It reduces some of the personal costs of getting involved—the cost of getting informed, for starters. The Internet is a peerless technology for personal research. Access to it enables an individual to find an abundance of information, in multimedia forms, at great convenience. News, documents, directories, discussions, tutorials: whatever the searcher deems worthwhile can be easily tagged or bookmarked for storage, retrieval, and return visits. In many cases, users can receive, upon request, automatic e-mail updates from the information provider.

I launched my quest by typing "airplane noise" into the search box at Google.com. It whisked back 55,800 leads, topped by a link to an airplane noise simulator and pages from documents and news articles I cared nothing about. I found the web site of the Metropolitan Washington Airports Authority and typed the same two-word phrase into its search box. Back came an error message: "*Airplane* was not found—please check your spelling." I clicked back to Google, tried "airplane noise opposition," and found the Noise Pollution Clearinghouse, which led me to U.S. Citizens Aviation Watch, a national association.

I had never heard of Aviation Watch, but then again, there were 23,000 national associations listed in the 1990 *Encyclopedia of Associations*.[2] This group said it lobbied for the Quiet Communities Act, a bill that would shift some responsibility for noise abatement from the Federal Aviation Administration (a prisoner of the airline business, according to the group) to the Environmental Protection Agency. That struck me as potentially worthwhile but did nothing for me now. The home page urged me to contact my local chapter, listed in the hyperlinked directory under "Virginia—Reagan Washington National." The chapter was called "Citizens for the Abatement of Aircraft Noise," at www.caan.org.

Bingo. I did not have to forge a coalitional wheel to advance my cause; CAAN had been rolling for thirteen years. Its web site had all the information I needed to become well versed on the issue. One page explained how noise is measured, so that I could decipher technical charts. A bulletin board and a quarterly newsletter, *Rumblings*, told me what the *Post* did not. An interactive flight simulator gave me controls for path, engine type, climb, and speed; as I took off from National, I could see the noise I was making in the form of concentric circles appearing on a map of the D.C. area, color-coded by decibel level. Very cool.

In keeping with one of the Internet's most exquisite political qualities, the information massaging my brain shared the screen with
opportunities for me to take online action. CAAN's web site sported
an e-mail center with contact information for officials, a plea for citizen data collection, and a downloadable page for contributions (with
a promise that online contributions would soon be an option). I liked
www.caan.org most of all because it exhibited the bright, cheerful,
scrappy tone—all right, the caan-do spirit—of the committed citizen–
activist:

> Please note: calls to the noise complaint lines will not
> decrease noise in and of themselves; but when there are
> *enough* complaints, elected officials at all levels can bring
> pressure to bear to change the situation.[3]

After a shaky start, my keyword-guided research had proved to be
up to the task. CAAN could serve as an outlet for my outrage. But
would anything come from my writing a check, subscribing to *Rumblings*, and answering the group's calls to action? I doubted it. For
CAAN neither displayed, nor showed signs of privately possessing, the
sorts of strategic and tactical information I knew to be essential to win
a political fight.

When and where was the next relevant public policy decision going
to be made? What was the best guess at the voting outcome? If it was
unfavorable, what sorts of pressure might swing enough votes to our
side to prevail? If that pressure could not be brought to bear, how
could we stall for more time, or switch the decision to a more favor-
able venue? Answers to these sorts of questions generally cannot be
found on the Web. They remain within closed circles, accessible, in
effect, only to those with the correct password.

Political messages still in development stay on the password-protected and encrypted areas of the Internet, and their most sensitive
aspects stay offline altogether. As sublime a source of keyword-
indexed intelligence as it is, the Web is too public a place for details
that might need to stay confidential for purposes of surprise and, it
must be admitted, deception. Anything I, as a citizen policy maker,
can see on the Web, anyone else can, too. I can spread the word about
a recommended or impending action with the "forward" button, and
so can anyone to whom I forward the word. Therefore, until a cam-

paign has determined who will say what to whom, when, and through which channels, certain information must be kept among those who can be trusted not to share it with the press or the opposition.

Keyword intelligence can tell me a lot about what just happened in politics, but password intelligence enables me to do something about what might happen next. With CAAN's online aid, I could learn about noise abatement at National Airport. But the web site lacked an "advisory board" roster of power players. It did not send out "action alerts" to marshal support just before an upcoming public policy decision. My call to the phone number listed went unreturned. This suggested to me that CAAN consisted of one, and possibly more, scientific experts and passionately concerned citizens, but no one with the acumen and power to execute a political strategy.

Keyword intelligence was not going to be enough to make a difference against Senator McCain, who soon announced his candidacy for president as someone who was going to clean up the corrupting influence of money in politics.

The Hunt for Inside Help

I wanted McCain's airport initiative stopped. It would not be easy. I had to find the password-protected know-how to (1) inject a message into the political system and (2) have that message spread through the system in such a way as to persuade John McCain to (3) recalculate the costs and benefits he would incur in pushing his proposals, if not (4) reconsider their public worth altogether. I lacked the temperament and ambition to venture offline, acquire this intelligence, and become a player myself, so I needed an insider or two to adopt my cause as their own. I could use the Net to hunt for them, but identifying the correct insiders would not be easy, either. Players in the policy making arena communicate about ongoing political controversies with nuance, preserving their capacity to shift positions as well as the confidentiality of their campaign deliberations.

I lacked the funds to hire a lobbyist. Someday, the Internet might permit me to multiply the force of my small disposable income by bundling it with those of strangers who shared my goal. Better yet, as a cybergroup, we could communicate regularly with our commissioned lobbyist as members of conventional interest groups do not. But today is not that day. An organization called www.lobbyforme.com already exists. It boasts a roster of twelve former members of Congress "whose broad experience, extensive knowledge, and contacts equip them to get results for you." But Lobbyforme doesn't yet allow visitors to select their own issues or develop their positions in concert with other citizens and the political agent(s) with whom they have contracted. Other Internet firms, such as Grassroots Enterprises (né Grassroots.com), aspire to develop and profit from an omnibus online advocacy apparatus. But they could not get me past step 1, at best.

It was time to think Madisonian and to look for an elected representative or two to take the fight to McCain. I could start with my own representatives, but there was no need to stop there. The Internet puts all elected officials on Earth within (theoretically) easy reach. Surely one of them could act proficiently on my behalf.

I am a registered voter in Arlington County. In Virginia, county and city governments are contiguous, not congruent. It is an extremely well-run county, and prides itself as the high-tech birthplace of DARPA, the Defense Department agency that was home to a predecessor to the Internet. So I knew that the five members of the County Board would read and respond to my e-mails. Fortunately, as www.co.arlington.va.us informed me, Barbara Favola, a Board member since 1997, chaired the Metropolitan Washington Council of Government's Committee on Noise Abatement at National and Dulles Airports. News clips quoted her as being on my side. I wanted to impress her from the start, and thus continued my research before contacting her.

The COG-CONANDA (yes, that's their acronym) web page at www.mwcog.org was the obverse of CAAN's site: sparse keyword intelligence, with whiffs of password intelligence. The page dared me, in effect, to show up at a meeting to learn who else was on the committee and whether its members' stature and its public–private composition as an independent nonprofit association endowed it with sufficient political power to compensate for its lack of constitutional, electoral, and legislative authority. The MWAA, in contrast, though also a regional body, was a statutory child of the United States Congress and the Commonwealth of Virginia.

As it was, the next meeting of Favola's committee was two months away. I went up the federal ladder to the office of my congressman, James P. Moran. His web site offered no help, but I had a nice telephone conversation with Tim Aiken of his staff. Aiken referred me to Favola, CAAN, and Neil Phillips, the calm airport complaint catcher guy. That made me feel as though I had done my homework. Aiken told me that he had received reports of planes powering up and idling on the tarmac, a phenomenon I knew as a passenger but had not considered in connection with my noise woes. He suggested that I become an "alert complainer" to the FAA. He also suggested contacting the Arizona news media to give them a fresh story angle on McCain and America West. Yes, yes, I thought to myself, but what are you and your boss going to do?

What more could they do? Like Favola, Moran had spoken out on the issue and perhaps spoken with McCain. They were capable representatives, but they weren't on the Senate Commerce Committee. I did not try to contact anyone in the offices of my senators or governor. I did not think that would get me any further.

I had a third option besides elected representatives and hired lobbyists: networking. American sages from Benjamin Franklin on have counseled that a secret of success is cultivating what sociologist Mark Granovetter has called "weak ties." A weak tie is an acquaintance not likely to share many of your tastes, views, and passions—but who may, precisely because your orbits intersect narrowly, be able to clue you in to something or someone you would not have come across on your own. In the digital age, we may amend the nomenclature and refer to such persons as "weak links."

During the time of my civic quest, I dropped my cause into many a conversation. At a baby shower for a friend of my wife, I took the card of a union official who worked with administrators at National Airport. At a conference on Internet politics, my "minirant" kindled feelings of solidarity from someone I see regularly on this conference circuit, someone who, as it turned out, also lived beneath a flight path. I did not know when or for what specific purpose I would recontact these individuals, but I thought it important to start a list. The Internet, I knew, could help me communicate with the people whose names were on that list.

Some individuals occupy nodal positions in the great civic web. They might not be able to help directly, but they take pride in having great numbers of acquaintances and in being able to put one in touch with exactly the right person who can be of assistance. We rely on these flesh-and-blood O'Hare Airports when we need jobs and dates.

Even when we do not seek them out, they often cross our paths, and the ensuing conversation glides, as if by magic, to topics on which they can put their connections to our good use.[4]

I cannot swear to it, but I think Trevor Potter, a coauthor of chapter 5 of this book, is one of these sorts of people. Now and then he mails out, to weak links such as me, a packet of articles he has enjoyed reading. One day, during a business lunch with him, I learned that he was counsel to the McCain for President campaign. Just like that, I was potentially one person away from The Man.

During our lunch, I sparred lightly with Trevor over the noise issue. I could not persuade him that the regional consensus and governing plan lifted my concerns above NIMBYism,[5] and he could not persuade me that the senator was simply advancing free-market principles. Dessert arrived. Trevor said, "Look, Mike, if you really want to solve your problem, you ought to support McCain for President. That will get him off the Senate Commerce Committee."

I could not argue with that logic. I liked Trevor and agreed with him on many issues. I admired much else about McCain. However, ensuring that the jet noise around my house would not worsen did not seem to be a sufficient rationale to support a presidential campaign. Furthermore, I preferred McCain to Bush but not to Bradley or Gore, and therefore I wanted Bush to win the Republican nomination over McCain, because I believed that would help the Democrats. So I had to banish the presidential race from consideration.

But Trevor's clever invocation of it disoriented me. Here I was, an eager activist, lost in a three-dimensional multitiered matrix of policy interests, government jurisdictions, and social sets. The local level had been a fine place to start, I thought, since my disturbed living condition was the proximate source of my civic itch. But the constitutional dispersion of authority removed a great deal of power from local grasp. The official bodies tasked to handle the problem were regional, and their semiadequate capacity to manage things was being stymied at the national level.

Viewed from another angle, the issue raised by my local situation was global. Noise is a form of pollution. CAAN informed me that the airlines were polluting the waters near National Airport by dumping de-icing fluid. The air was being polluted, too. This implied that joining an environmental movement as wide as the web might be a good move. But I knew no weak link who could direct me toward specific representation on that level.

I grew frustrated. Every issue entails other issues. Every U.S. government body with jurisdiction on an issue shares that jurisdiction with other bodies. Every citizen who takes a position on an issue to a body meets other people with different takes on the issue. It is a matrix to daunt Keanu Reeves. In my Internet perambulations, I had put on blinders, pushing past links to other levels, concerns, and perspectives to make progress. In all likelihood, I had missed something. Perhaps I should have looked into the coalition behind the Quiet Communities Act. Perhaps I should have worked harder at developing my own list of contacts. Perhaps I should have explored legal options—not that lawyers come any cheaper than lobbyists. What I did, instead, was reflect on the challenges individuals like me faced.

A Motivational Morphology

Getting smart turns out to be one of several behavioral prerequisites to civic participation. (See the chapter 8 discussion on how civic education matters more than technology in closing the so-called digital divide, and the chapter 9 discussion on the social distribution of civic knowledge.) Besides knowledge, most scholars agree that attention, interest, and a sense of efficacy are also necessary. On each factor, the advent of the Internet affects the motivation of citizens to be involved in public life in contradictory ways.

As I learned from my adventure, the Internet supplies keyword intelligence in abundance but little, if any, password intelligence. Knowing that feature of online information is a crucial piece of civic knowledge. With respect to paying attention to politics, again the Net helps and hurts. It takes less time for an individual to acquire information online than through other communication channels; similar efficiencies are obtained with respect to sending messages to others as part of a campaign. But the Internet places more information options before the eye. That action alert you send is going to be one of dozens of e-mails in someone's in-box. Even when people add more time into their days to spend online by subtracting hours formerly spent watching television—a trend documented in recent polling, especially among youth—the complex structure of politics and society makes it likely that they will get sidetracked.[6] Thus, attention (or eyeballs, in

Net lingo) shapes up as the great limiting factor for a medium with several infinite communications dimensions.

Having an interest means more than just awareness of a political problem or opportunity: There must also be imaginable and meaningful stakes associated with the possibility of public engagement. Had I adopted the attitude that nothing could be done about the jet noise, that would be a sign of lack of interest, in this sense of the term. The Internet can excite the civic imagination by making it easy for those with Internet access to see a problem that affects them and then to send a political message about it. But this is not as meaningful a route of influence as it may seem at first. Precisely because an e-mail to Congress or the newspaper is so easy, it is usually regarded as a minimal sign of interest, first by the message recipients and then, in time, by the senders. Civic interest must be sustained in the face of disappointing user sessions.

A sense of efficacy—the sense that one can win—derives from self-esteem and is reinforced by prior victories, positive interim results, and morale boosts from others. The Internet, with its incomparable capacity to provide instant and detailed feedback, holds out terrific potential as a poster of results. But Internet interactions are too impersonal to pick up one's spirits when the results are discouraging or, more likely, unclear. The Internet can nourish a personal sense of efficacy indirectly, in that the anonymity it offers may assuage the fear of public embarrassment. Many people recoil at the prospect of entering the public square, afraid of reprisals and doubtful of the adequacy of their skills. However, anonymity opens a box of complications, as chapter 1 in this book discusses. The decision to disclose one's true identity becomes part of the political calculus. For example, the longer a civic participant remains masked, the more cumbersome it becomes to revise or reveal the public self, unless the anonymity attracts such attention as a stunt that the unmasking will make big news (as with the author of the novel *Primary Colors*).

My motivation on my noise project varied. It rose with the noise and with the news about McCain. It fell as I saw myself lost in the matrix. On February 29, 2000, I passed on the opportunity to switch my party registration at the voting booth, declining to cast a mischievous ballot for John McCain in the Virginia primary. On March 7, "Super Tuesday," as McCain's presidential candidacy flickered out, congressional negotiators agreed on a provision to expand by twenty-four the number of flights in and out of Ronald Reagan Washington National Airport. Twelve of the flights would be permitted to exceed the 1,250-mile limit imposed on incoming flights to National. On July 5, Transportation Secretary Rodney Slater announced that America West had been awarded three of the twelve long-distance flight slots. My cause was now, officially, lost.

Up for the Count

My civic odyssey poses a challenge of democratic design. How can the Internet be arranged to enhance citizen involvement in public policy making?[7] And who will make the arrangements?

There have been a few dazzling online finesses of the matrix. For a couple of years, a family of web sites allowed people to join campaigns to eliminate hunger, save rain forests, and care for children with AIDS around the world with just one free click per day. (Advertisers paid for the food, acreage, and professional attention, respectively, in exchange for the marketing opportunity to show site visitors their logos after they clicked.) But realism bids us not to rely solely on bypassing the political system. It reminds us that password intelligence, which is essential to success with politics on the Internet, will not surface online except by mistake. And realism asks us not to pretend that direct democracy (voting, town meetings), although an essential component of a good political system, could ever replace—even in part, and even with the help of the Internet—the representative, juridical, and administrative processes that constitute our contemporary government.

Yet one precept of realism for much of the twentieth century may be discarded. It is that citizens must be "omni-competent" for democracy to exist, a major presumption of Walter Lippmann's 1922 masterwork of political communication theory, *Public Opinion*. Lippmann argued that no one could assimilate all the information needed to participate rationally in public affairs. He advised Americans to relinquish the dream of democratic government and to adopt in its place a modernized system in which experts play a crucial role:

> [T]he outsider, and every one of us is an outsider to all but a few aspects of modern life, has neither time, nor attention, nor interest, nor the equipment for specific judgment. It is

on the men inside, working under conditions that are sound, that the daily administrations of society must rest.[8]

The Internet *per se* does not negate Lippmann's thesis about the average citizen's capacity for democratic politics. Instead, the hope that citizens can contribute to democratic government in more than just symbolic ways gains credence from another theory grounded in social psychology. As exemplified in Samuel Popkin's work *The Reasoning Voter*, this new theory argues that citizens can be rational without being fully involved, so long as they rely on the right kinds of "information shortcuts" when they act:

> [L]ow-information rationality, or "gut" rationality, best describes the kind of practical reasoning about government and politics in which people actually engage. [It] is by no means devoid of substantive content, and is instead a process that economically incorporates learning and information from past experiences, daily life, the media, and political campaigns.[9]

Knowing which party a candidate belongs to is a common information shortcut. Recognizing the name of a trusted individual or organization on an endorsement list is another.

Because voters use information shortcuts to choose among candidates, and because online shortcuts of the political system enable volunteers to make a difference in the world, it seems feasible to call for a combination that fosters greater citizen participation in policy making. (By "greater," I mean both more people and more effective.) I think the creation of "civic participation counters" offers just such a combination of psychological appeal and technological prowess.

The Internet has spawned a profusion of real-time counters, some quite popular and profitable. Amazon.com displays up-to-the-minute sales totals, spurring the friends of a first-time author to move their buddy up the list hundreds of thousands of places in a matter of hours. The company eBay displays auction bids, electrifying its virtual flea market with the excitement of a competition. Political advocates seeking popular support in a democratically responsible manner can devise counting categories and computing algorithms that would make policy activism more legible, authentic, appealing, and effective: One click to participate, another click to see one's participation show up in the running totals, a third click to see the current process in a historical or hortatory (Just one thousand more and we reach our goal!) context.

In a groundbreaking study of American-style policy making, John Kingdon postulated that every successful advocacy campaign combines a definition of the problem with a workable solution and a formidable coalition of supporters.[10] One type of counter, then, could tabulate testimony to the existence of a problem requiring a political solution. I know I would be a more alert complainer if I could turn to a web site and see my complaint about airplane noise added to a total—and know, further, that authorities would see that total, too. The cumulative count, and exceptionally high daily counts ("spikes" in the graph), could make news.

A second type of counter could keep track of those in support of a particular solution to a problem: Here is a list of who joined the opposition to McCain this week; there's the neighborhood-by-neighborhood breakdown, overlaid on the flight path map. A third counter type could track the expansion of the coalition behind the problem's solution: How many members of the Virginia, Maryland, and District of Columbia delegations have pledged to support us? What about local businesses, unions, associations, and other community institutions located within the flight path area? Another coalition's counter could spell out the disbursement of its political capital, especially dollars and volunteer hours. Prior to allocation, participants could indicate their preferences; the actual allocation would remain an offline process, but the results could be posted after those decisions were implemented.

Online counters would encourage middle-class, overeducated moderates like me, dissatisfied with the existing channels of civic participation. I vote regularly, but my voting choices are almost always out of sync and out of touch with my policy preferences. I grasp enough of the intricacies of power politics to know that, as with the stock market, being an occasional player would leave me worse off than paying for a professional to handle my portfolio. But I cannot afford a professional agent for politics. In the past few years, I have been quoted frequently in the news as an expert on online politics, but that slot is not wide enough for my personal political views. Opinion polls sometimes make my views semivisible, in that I can see what percentage of a population falls into an answer category that bears a rough correspondence to what I would say on the subject, if asked. But polls do not allow me to make my views on policy matters audible, as in "This is what I want to see happen."

I am a sporadic and self-conscious citizen. I have nothing to show for my efforts at getting involved besides this story. But political science data show that I am still more engaged in public life than most Americans.[11] The social practice of talking about politics constructively has, in one scholar's apt description, evaporated.[12] Online participation counters would not be a panacea. But they would demand little time. They would not make wild promises about the impact of a tabulated action. If well constructed, they would be neither too complex to be understood by most people nor too simplistic to pervert or thwart a cause. Had counters existed in my case, they would have given me something concrete: a personal and public record of my civic activities in the context of a real policy dispute. They would have documented my standing up and being counted.

Counters are a realistic possibility, because online strategists and their advocacy group clients have incentives to create them. The counters would provide fast and precise feedback data. Therefore, even if they did not, of themselves, increase grassroots support, they would help a campaign by adding to its managers' knowledge of how it was faring. Strategists could make adjustments and construct public narratives of a political controversy. Their narratives, in turn, could lead citizens to act based on high-quality information shortcuts. (A high-quality shortcut justifies an action in terms of political structure, instead of personality or scandal.[13]) I was reminded of the need for high-quality shortcuts when I was at home one day at 3:59 in the afternoon, the time America West flight 45 departed Washington National on its nonstop journey to Phoenix. The airplane noise stimulus should have prompted me to stay involved, not to get mad at McCain.

Obstacles await makers of civic participation counters. Like all online campaigners, they have to find ways of ensuring individual privacy, public authenticity, and insider accuracy all at once. William Galston's concern (voiced in chapter 3 of this book) about how the Internet might exacerbate the civic dysfunctions of a compartmentalized populace must be addressed; broad-based coalitions with diverse memberships should be a major goal of an online civic entrepreneur.

But these obstacles are not worth surmounting. Citizen involvement in public policy making builds individual character, generates social trust, and steers the state in the direction of both rational governance and political justice.

If you agree, click here.

Notes

1. The official name is now Ronald Reagan Washington National Airport. Locals such as me who had no input in the change continue to call it by the old name.

2. Theda Skocpol, "Advocates Without Members: The Recent Transformation of American Civic Life," in *Civic Engagement in American Democracy*, ed. Theda Skocpol and Morris P. Fiorina (Washington, D.C.: Brookings Institution Press, 1999).

3. www.caan.org/gripe.html.

4. Malcolm Gladwell, "Six Degrees of Lois Weisberg," *The New Yorker*, 11 January 1999.

5. NIMBY stands for "Not In My Back Yard," the stereotypical slogan of narrow-minded homeowners.

6. Pew Research Center for the People and the Press, *Internet Sapping Broadcast News Audience*, news release, 11 June 2000, www.people-press.org.

7. This seems the appropriate place to call attention to limits on the scope of this essay. I have not thought through the implications of my argument and recommendations for other settings of democratic citizenship: the campaign trail and the voting booth; the town hall; the negotiating table; the courtroom; the streets; and, beyond the public sphere, the myriad locations of everyday life. ("Democracy," E. B. White wrote in "Notes and Comment," *The New Yorker*, 3 July 1943, "is the 'don't' in 'don't shove.'") Nor do I take up here the matter of adequate resources for civic participation; my argument and recommendations are pitched to middle-class levels of literacy, health, income, and safety, which millions of Americans have, sadly, not yet attained, as chapter 8 and chapter 9 document.

8. Walter Lippmann, *Public Opinion* (New York, The Free Press, 1965), 251.

9. Samuel L. Popkin, *The Reasoning Voter: Communication and Persuasion in Presidential Campaigns*, (Chicago, Ill.: University of Chicago Press, 1991), 212.

10. John W. Kingdon, *Agendas, Alternatives, and Public Policies*, 2nd ed. (New York: Harper Collins Publishers, 1995).

11. Sidney Verba, Kay Lehman Schlozman, and Henry E. Brady, *Voice and Equality: Civic Voluntarism in American Politics* (Cambridge, Mass.: Harvard University Press, 1995).

12. Nina Eliasoph, *Avoiding Politics: How Americans Produce Apathy in Everyday Life* (New York: Cambridge University Press, 1999).

13. Samuel L. Popkin and Michael A. Dimick, "Political Knowledge and Citizen Competence," in *Citizen Competence and Democratic Institutions*, ed. Stephen L. Elkin and Koral Edward Soltan (University Park, Pa.: Pennsylvania State University Press, 1999).

Civic Participation and Technology Inequality: The "Killer Application" Is Education

8

ANTHONY G. WILHELM

T**ALK DURING THE** 1990s of connecting every household and institution to the Internet as the fulfillment of a bold democratic vision has given way at the beginning of this decade to a stark realization: the development of new hardware applications alone, regardless of how slick or fast, will be unlikely to move all people toward the information society's center. Recent years have witnessed the frenetic deployment of new information and communications services, including higher-speed conduits to transport video, data, and graphics and the development of more "magical" software applications. Government action, moreover, has largely tracked the path of industry policy, advancing solutions that focus on "boxes and wires," such as wiring schools and libraries. Although these infrastructure programs are vital and must be preserved and extended where appropriate, they will achieve only limited success in the absence of deeper commitments to training, education, and content development.

Decision makers trumpet their success in connecting millions of Americans to the network. This has been no small feat. Virtually all of the nation's schools and libraries have at least a single Internet connection; almost half of all households can access online services; workplaces offer e-mail accounts to millions of employees; and nonprofit community centers are mushrooming, with neighborhood residents availing themselves of computer applications and the Web. A decade of investment and the hottest economy on record, however, have not brought access to all Americans. According to the latest data, a digital divide continues unabated, with households on the margin still unlikely to be online into 2005 and beyond.[1] In remote areas of the country and among the very poor, service can be nonexistent. Tens of millions of U.S. residents remain on the periphery, complete strangers to the world of e-commerce, instant communications, and civic engagement.[2] A broadband technology divide also looms, in which new high-speed services, delivering video and voice over the Internet (including civic applications), threaten to marginalize millions of residents who may be unable to adopt these applications until well after the Internet has become a staple of civic and political life.[3] With information technology companies teetering and Wall Street investors increasingly diffident, the optimists of the late 1990s who forecasted the closing of the digital divide at the hands of the market are now yielding to more measured approaches to the issue.

Citizens cannot participate in e-democracy without Internet access. Thus, public- and private-sector vigilance and creative public policy are needed to ensure that no Americans are left behind. However, access is a necessary but not sufficient resolution to the problem of nonparticipation in online civic and political life. With the likelihood that many Americans will be excluded from civic engagement, advocacy, political organization, and electoral campaigning—perhaps through the 2004 and 2008 elections and beyond—the question arises, what are the "killer applications" that might close the gap between those near the center and the persons on the margins of public life? Our tendency might be to think about the faster, sleeker, and more portable services that will make life easier and better, as advertisers contend. Auctioning the so-called third-generation (3-G) wireless systems, for example, opens the door to a range of broadband services to be deployed that may, with accelerated processor speed and enhanced graphical displays, create hand-held tools many times more powerful than today's devices.[4] But will these new palm technologies be the killer applications a democracy seeks? Palm applications are already being introduced to students, many of whom are already familiar with the mechanics of their use, having grown up on Sony PlayStations and Nintendo Game Boys. However, can young people's enthusiasm for the technology be channeled toward civic applications, to strengthen their ties to the fragile civic web?

Having an Internet connection does not lead ineluctably to the navigation of the civic web any more than owning a car leads a citizen to the polling station on Election Day. Navigating online civic and political life depends on the possession of other capabilities that are often ignored in discussions of technology and democracy. Campaigns to extend the Internet's technical reach to strengthen democracy side-step an important condition: the possession of the resources, talents, and motivations to use the Web effectively and to apply these skills for civic and political purposes.[5] These skills are absorbed through formal and informal education (e.g., school attendance, apprenticeships, peer learning, family socialization, and public-spirited media messages). These forms of education underwrite a person's capacity to participate in the life of the community, whether on a face-to-face or electronic basis. Educational attainment has long been the mainsail powering civic participation.[6] It is also a primary variable explaining online access and use.[7] This chapter will explore the centrality of education—conceived broadly as formal and informal education, often called life-long learning—both in broadening the reach of emerging communications technologies, and in enhancing the possibility that these tools will be used for civic and political engagement.

The True Backbone of the Information Society

In telecommunications jargon, "backbone" infrastructure is a term describing the thick, high-capacity fiber-optic and cable trunks that crisscross the nation and are concentrated in high-density, mostly affluent, population areas. These fat pipes support the bulk of the heavy data traffic that eventually branches off and flows at various speeds to end users in homes, workplaces, and other institutions. Whereas experts often say that broadband deployment lies at the heart of the digital economy in spurring e-commerce and e-business, it is improbable that the political economy alone is sufficient to invigorate civic life, particularly in attracting marginal voices to come closer to the center of the public sphere. As hardware and bandwidth are useless without the capacity to exploit them, it is reasonable to posit that edu-cational development strengthens the value of the network's utility as a tool for democracy. In short, the rise of the information economy places a higher premium on lifelong learning as the process by which the network's potential can be more fully realized as, among other things, a tool for civic incorporation and reinvigoration. The true backbone architecture, then, is education and informal learning—as borne out by the available studies on the digital divide, the over-whelming majority of which demonstrate the importance of education in their explanations of the prevalence of Internet connectivity in American households.[8] The technologists have it backward: Educational attainment, along with family income, predicts the unequal deployment of high-speed wires. This true Internet backbone supports entire communities, which can return earnings to investors. But it bypasses other communities.

In a previous work I outlined a resource model of participation in the electronic civic sphere in which socioeconomic variables such as education were fleshed out as the set of resources and capacities anchoring participation in online public life.[9] This chapter explores the argument further, focusing on lifelong educational development as a core capacity in the fulfillment of expectations around universal civic and political participation in cyberspace. Whereas in much of the literature on the Internet and democracy, education is defined narrowly as formal educational attainment and understood as the completion of high school or college, this article explores broader lifelong learning activities that could spark Internet use for civic purposes.

Survey research and marketing data from recent studies of computer and Internet access and use reveal that education is a strong predictor of Internet connectivity. Although a household's income often drives its purchase of expensive hardware such as computers, other factors prevail in explaining monthly Internet subscriptions. When asked to give a reason for not accessing the Internet at home, a plurality of people respond that they "don't want it."[10] Respondents with relatively limited levels of educational attainment (less than a high school diploma) also provide this response over cost as the primary impediment to Internet access, suggesting that many householders currently cannot foresee sufficient utility in these information and communications tools to justify an investment in them.

Gaps in Internet access along educational lines continue to grow and define the digital divide, not only between college graduates and those without a high school diploma but also between college graduates and high school graduates. Between 1998 and 2000, the divide between those at the highest and lowest education levels increased almost 20 percent.[11] Figure 8.1 depicts the strong correlation between educational attainment and household Internet access, with virtually 70 percent of householders with a postgraduate degree hooked up to the Internet in 2000, compared with only about 12 percent of householders without a high school diploma. The further one steps down the rungs of educational attainment, the lower the percentage of Internet users, with American residents with minimal formal educational training barely registering on the radar screen of the information society. Another report shows that the usage difference between high school and college graduates grew between 1993 and 1997, largely due to the access growth among the most educated groups. These differences remain significant even when researchers account for income differences.[12] The late 1990s and the beginning of this decade portend a widening gap in Internet access and use because of the near saturation of affluent, highly educated households and the slow percolation of new telecommunications applications in households and communities with modest incomes and scant educational training.

The U.S. Department of Commerce data are supported by other recent national studies of Internet diffusion. A report from the Stanford Institute for the Quantitative Study of Society, for example, found that "by far the most important factors facilitating or inhibiting

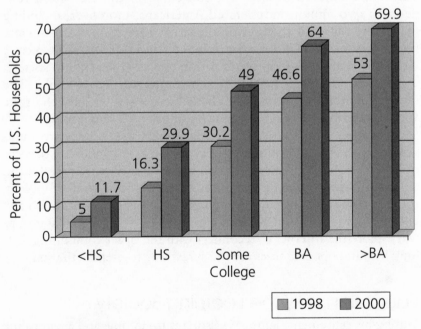

Figure 8.1.   Households with Internet Access

Source: U.S. Department of Commerce, Falling through the Net: Toward Digital Inclusion. Washington, D.C.: U.S. Department of Commerce, October 2000.

Internet access are education and age."[13] A college education boosts rates of Internet access by well over 40 percentage points compared to the least educated group. As the technologies diffuse, the generational divide will likely close. More Internet-savvy cohorts will replace older Americans who lag behind in adopting technology. It remains less clear how quickly the educational divide will close, as elementary and secondary education advancements, despite some gains, remain listless along certain indicators such as dropout rates, high school completion rates, reading proficiency, and school violence.[14]

Focusing intently on formal and informal lifelong learning by no means precludes attention to other factors that contribute to disenfranchisement. A litany of variables partly explains asymmetries in groups' abilities to access and use the Internet, variables such as occupational status, age, race, and ethnicity. Some groups remain on the periphery of the Internet society, such as the two million Native Americans for whom Internet access (particularly on tribal lands) remains a distant goal, as the presence of even basic infrastructure such as running water and telephony still elude many reservation residents.[15] Two million incarcerated Americans, moreover, including many who will find themselves alienated from mainstream society upon their release without some computer and Internet skills, receive virtually no opportunities to transition effectively back into society. Two-thirds of inmates have not even completed high school.[16] The disabled community faces formidable challenges, with much of the Web inaccessible to sight- and hearing-impaired Internet users.[17]

Education is by no means the magic bullet that will ensure a universally accessible and vigorous public Internet. A confluence of technological, policy, and basic infrastructure initiatives is critical. Still, although lifelong learning is not a sufficient solution to the problem, the data show that education stimulates both online participation and engagement in civic and political life. To ensure that marginal groups will explore the Internet to reconnect with the larger community, lifelong learning opportunities are the surest way to prepare the soil.

Education and the Learning Society

During his retirement, James Madison returned time and again to the interrelationship of education and community participation in safeguarding the virtue of self-government. In his 1822 letter to William

Barry regarding the Kentucky legislature's plan for the general diffusion of knowledge, Madison approved of the state's comprehensive and universal approach to education. Learned institutions, according to Madison, are necessary to cultivate "particular talents required for some of the Public Trusts, on the able execution of which the welfare of the people depends."[18] A sound educational system should impart the necessary skills for citizens to appraise the performance of representatives and partake of civic matters themselves. Madison also praised the universal nature of the system: that no youth, regardless of his or her class, should be overlooked in studying basic skills such as reading, writing, and arithmetic. In order to ensure that learners, particularly the poor, would not forsake education for amusements, Madison advocated the study of geography, travel, and the customs of nations in order to add entertainment to the rather dry rudiments of grammar and math.

Madison's letter captures many of the fundamentals of the learning society. It is anchored in the Enlightenment vision that diffusion of knowledge provides the surest means for effective self-government. Imparting universal literacy to all young people in a manner that is entertaining as well as edifying anticipates modern pedagogy and practice. Decision makers view education as the primary mechanism to convey the necessary skills for citizens to fulfill their individual life plans, enjoy a decent quality of life, and engage in what Madison calls "the common purposes of life."[19]

The language used to name the lifelong process of citizen self-improvement is only one thing that has changed. Madison's vision of democratic life may also be more difficult to instill now than in his day. Ironically, the widespread diffusion of communications media may hurt, more than help, the cause. Although teenagers consume media for five to seven hours per day, there is little to guarantee that the confluence of these activities bears any positive correlation to public engagement, let alone educational achievement.[20] Teens use media to watch entertainment programs, talk to friends on the telephone, participate in commercial chat rooms, and download music files.

Unfortunately, the currency of the learning society has been devalued at a time when its bolstering is urgently needed. The public has taken to the Internet like children to Pokémon cards, inaugurating a sort of media narcissism in which the exploits of the Internet are continuously reflected in newspapers, magazines, and the electronic media. Of course, the majority of seemingly objective suppliers of news about the Net have vested interests in the growth of the technology sector.[21] The bland politics at the beginning of this century, moreover, address simple problems and peddle watered-down solutions in league with media confederates.[22] For example, the constant wrangling between conservatives and liberals over the U.S. Department of Education (particularly around a multibillion-dollar school construction program) at a time when monies can be found for technology-related projects highlights this unsettling tendency to eschew addressing big problems in favor of quick fixes. The nation's investment in hardware and telecommunications services, such as telephone and Internet connections, has been in the billions of dollars in K–12 schools. Federal policy has been bullish on infrastructure deployment and overly demure on human-capital development.

It is clear today that education is more than formal school training. It encompasses the constellation of formal and informal learning opportunities that unfold before citizens in the course of their lifetimes. A focus on a learning society points to education as the linchpin of self-improvement and a necessary component, as Madison suggested, for executing our responsibilities in civic and political society. A virtuous circle can be conceptualized to shed light on the interrelationship of lifelong learning, the adoption or use of emerging information and communications technologies such as the Internet, and the use of these tools for civic purposes.

Figure 8.2 depicts the interrelationship of four conditions that seem fundamental in moving society stepwise toward fuller participation in e-democracy.

Critical attention to lifelong learning opportunities and public education leads to a more robust demand for telecommunications services. This demand translates not only in the proclivity to purchase and own products and services such as computers and Internet connections, but also to seek out publicly available resources found in libraries, schools, and community centers. Research shows that even the most modest experience with and exposure to computer applications and the Internet under the right circumstances generates self-efficacy, self-esteem, and an active involvement in the creation of knowledge.[23] Unlike television—a medium that broadcasts messages to a passive public in the hopes of motivating people to purchase products or vote for candidates—the Internet in the right context invites a

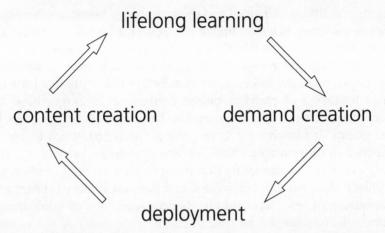

Figure 8.2.   The Virtuous Circle of Education's Role in Technology Adoption and Use for Civic Purposes

constructive role for citizens. The mobilization of civil society during the World Trade Organization meetings in late 1999 in Seattle, for example, intimates the Internet's power as a lever for social change, motivating citizens to develop their own web sites or join listservs or to send e-mails to power brokers. This sort of catalytic event generates centripetal forces within the virtuous circle—in particular, inspiring citizens to view the Internet as a productive and democratic force for social change.

The civic use of the Internet—for advocacy, online organizing, electoral participation, or searching for candidate information—depends in large measure on the presence of antecedent resources, the best proxy for which is formal educational attainment. Informal contexts for nurturing political skills also help explain civic engagement, such as the political impact of certain Protestant denominations in cultivating opportunities to exercise politically relevant skills, particularly among African Americans.[24] The growth of lifelong learning opportunities increases the likelihood that prospective Internet users will find in the technology a viable way to address their needs. Because there seems to be no substitute for providing exposure to and experience with the Internet in generating demand for civic content, it is critical that policies be in place to increase Internet access, particularly in public access centers, in order to spread the benefits of the technology. As lifelong learning is enhanced and the technology becomes ubiquitous, citizens are more likely to utilize this resource and to fulfill more of their learning needs online, thus reinforcing the virtuous circle.

Increasingly, the mantra both of domestic and international development vis-à-vis the information society spotlights the need for universal literacy and edifying online content to leverage these new telecommunications and Internet-based resources.[25] Yet, as Peter Levine points out in chapter 4, in general the Internet reinforces the influence of those whose voices are already amplified in society. Thus arises the central legitimating question of advanced democracies: how to universalize participation in civic and political affairs to ensure a fair distribution of resources and life chances regardless of one's starting conditions. Sustained attention to the four elements of the virtuous circle is critical to initiate the participation of persons on the fringes of society in the electronic public sphere. Tackling any particular variable in isolation leads to the possible attenuation of the civic web; ignoring human-capacity building in particular stymies the civic web's potential.

Public Schools, Community Centers, and Media Institutions: Incubators of the Civic Web

According to Robert Putnam, among others, the nadir of civic engagement has been reached in present-day America. We have become our own grave diggers, the victims of unplanned growth that fetters freedom of movement, and of a national addiction to solipsistic media that clutches our attention in the evenings away from more neighborly pursuits.[26] For Putnam the Internet provides little solace, as cyberspace for all intents and purposes probably replicates the anomie of the nonvirtual world, offering "a niftier telephone or a niftier television."[27] This dyspeptic appraisal of early twenty-first century America offers little consolation in the way of reforming *media* institutions to protect democracy. Because Americans—particularly younger Americans—spend so much time consuming media of one sort or another, solutions to civic apathy that do not address media use and reform are as effectual as preventive measures against lung cancer that do not address smoking. This section will focus on the intersection of public schools, community centers, and media outlets as institutions that can help strengthen the fabric of the civic web, because these are arenas in which motivation is kindled and capabilities are developed. *Public schools* are a fulcrum for inculcating civic education and universal literacy. Other institutions quench the learning needs of people for whom formal educational institutions are impractical or insufficient. *Community centers* have multiplied in recent years, as welcoming spaces in which youth and adults alike can access the Internet and oftentimes can meet a range of learning needs in a safe and flexible environment. Nonprofit workforce development programs have sprung up across the nation, addressing the needs of underskilled adults who require some knowledge of information technology to seize even entry-level employment opportunities.[28] Mentoring programs are sparking the curiosity of young people in disadvantaged neighborhoods who have perhaps dropped out of school or require a nontraditional approach to draw them into a technology-mediated learning environment.[29] As the poet Yeats is widely credited with saying, learning is not the filling of a pail but the lighting of a fire, and young people often need mentors to help them design and construct their own learning environments, including their experiences with civic life. *Media institutions* are also critical in setting ambient expectations around civic engagement. Media influence the attitudes and behaviors of citizens from the time one awakes in the morning to the cacophony of talk radio to the sleek news and entertainment formats of the evening. Media partly frame a citizen's orientation toward public life.

Public schools face a Herculean challenge in integrating technology effectively into the learning environment. Most teachers do not feel comfortable using technology in the classroom, and it is uncommon for instructors to harness the Internet for constructivist learning. According to the National Center for Education Statistics, in 1999 only 32 percent of teachers in the poorest schools used computers or the Internet a great deal to create instructional materials, compared with 52 percent in the wealthiest schools. Those teachers with the greatest access to professional development opportunities felt the most prepared to use instructional technology in their teaching.[30]

In terms of achieving greater equality in students' opportunity to learn, technological innovation often drives a deeper wedge between information haves and have-nots. Thus, less affluent districts are often playing catch-up to cohorts with higher per-pupil expenditures. In 1999, there were seven students per instructional computer with Internet access in districts with less than 11 percent of students in poverty, compared with sixteen per computer in schools with poverty levels over 71 percent.[31] Only 39 percent of instructional rooms had Internet access in the highest-poverty public schools in 1998, compared with 62 percent of lowest-poverty public schools. More troubling, the gap actually increased between 1998 and 1999, with lowest-poverty schools increasing to 74 percent of instructional rooms connected and highest-poverty instructional rooms holding steady at 39 percent.[32]

While schools scramble to train teachers and deploy a modern communications infrastructure, they risk falling behind more nimble institutions that can experiment with the use of technology for civic engagement. The Center for Democracy and Citizenship at the University of Minnesota and the New York City-based Libraries for the Future are poised to pilot an innovative model of youth engagement, centering on the use of new information technology for public works projects, called the Community Information Corps (CIC). The mission of CIC is to channel young people's enthusiasm for the Internet into fulfilling civic needs, including youth-oriented civic journalism and what founder Harry Boyte calls "public works": projects taken on for public purposes and in public ways, such as the creation of Web publishing to explore community identity.[33]

These strategies to reengage youth in civic activities using new technology are rooted in local contexts, underscoring the importance of local action in sustaining democratic praxis. Although youths will ultimately share their civic experiences worldwide via the technology just as seamlessly as they can now swap music files, the initial experience is intensely local. Young people in low-income communities and ethnic enclaves are particularly important targets of CIC. Understanding and appreciating diversity are core values of civic-mindedness, yet diversity is often eschewed on the Web, due to the Web's anonymity and text-based interface.

Two of the challenges in ensuring the success of models such as CIC are sustainability and scale. It is expensive to jump-start even one program, given the technology and staff-intensive nature of these activities. Programs that begin with seed money from a private foundation or other grant maker find that the well dries up without a sustainability model. Taking pilot initiatives to scale is problematic, as large-scale funding streams are rare in today's political climate unless one is developing a commercial venture. Here, the media can play a crucial role. Because media can broadcast (or netcast) to large audiences, they can help build demand for public-interest technology applications. For example, a current public service announcement campaign produced by the Kaiser Family Foundation aims to motivate disadvantaged youths of color to flock to community centers to get connected to the Internet. Of course, the purposes for which youth will apply their newfound skills remains undisciplined—youths being youths—and thus there is a need for mentors, programs, lifelong learning opportunities, and edifying content that tie together the processes of technology adoption and civic engagement.

Media Reform in the Service of Democracy

It is highly likely that civic and political engagement will migrate to the Internet, perhaps imperceptibly, so that campaigning, advocacy, voting, and volunteering will find their center of gravity online rather than on television or even in face-to-face venues. It will soon be second nature for civic-minded students, raised on the Internet, to participate in faraway environmental crusades or indigenous peoples' movements through cyberspace. This vision of the not-too-distant future could be quite powerful if it becomes a priority for decision makers across the globe to ensure that every community has access to the Internet and that new information and communications tools are leveraged with the necessary investment in lifelong learning and human-capacity development.

It is a big *if*. Because most media, with the exception of broadcast, remain largely unregulated, it is difficult to salvage mediated civic practice from the ravages of commercialization without intervention. Media in the service of public purposes will either be consumed by the commercial sector or will effectively disappear, marginalized by the referral systems and search engines of new media companies that cue information not according to the needs of citizens but according to the dictates of advertisers.[34]

Bold action is needed in terms of (1) obligating commercial media actors to serve the interests of democracy, not just shareholders, and

(2) generating an endowment from media companies to serve the life-long learning needs of the American public.[35] On the first of these propositions, the role of government in ensuring that broadcasting and new media outlets serve the public interest is critical, given the paucity of public affairs and educational programming available on commercial networks.[36] One recent study showed that during a partic-ular fortnight, only 0.3 percent of programming on the commercial networks was dedicated to locally produced public affairs program-ming.[37] Commercial attention to lifelong learning programming is also largely nonexistent. Concerning the second proposition, commu-nities clearly need resources to produce their own content and to see their own interests and aspirations mirrored in community media, whether through local community Web portals, ethnic newspapers, low-power radio or cable access television.[38] The process of creating these resources through a lifelong-learning endowment—grown from assets on the sale, transfer, and auctioning of media companies and of the portion of the electromagnetic spectrum earmarked for telecom-munications services—would provide a significant pool of funds to develop viable alternatives to the current commercial media.

These propositions require a degree of public awareness and engagement in communications policy that has rarely surfaced. The public in general has very little knowledge of how media are regulated, see these as low-salience issues, and have low expectations for how the media should serve civic needs. The good news, however, is that edu-cation is the important wedge issue to invite the public to explore media reform questions. An overwhelming majority of the public sup-ports additional media obligations to meet the nation's educational needs.[39] In this important sense, educational policy greets media and telecommunications policy in serving the learning and civic needs of the nation.

Notes

1. Jupiter Research, *Income and Age, Not Ethnicity, to Remain Largest Gap for U.S. Digital Divide*, jup.com/company/pressrelease.jsp?doc=pr000615, 20 Dec. 2000.

2. U.S. Department of Commerce, *Falling through the Net: Toward Digital Inclusion* (Washington, D.C.: U.S. Department of Commerce, 2000).

3. Jupiter Research, *More Than One in Three US Online Households Will*

Connect Via Broadband in 2005, jup.com/company/pressrelease.jsp?doc =pr001101, 20 Dec. 2000.

4. Federal Communications Commission, *Third Generation (3G) Wireless*, www.fcc.gov/3G/, 20 Dec. 2000.

5. Amartya Sen, *Development as Freedom* (New York: Alfred A. Knopf, 1999), 38–40.

6. Sidney Verba, Kay Lehman Schlozman, and Henry E. Brady, *Voice and Equality: Civic Voluntarism in American Politics* (Cambridge, Mass.: Harvard University Press, 1995), 433.

7. C. Richard Neu, Robert H. Anderson, and Tora K. Bikson, *Sending Your Government a Message: E-mail Communication Between Citizens and Government* (Santa Monica, Calif.: RAND, 1999), 131–34.

8. Norman H. Nie and Lutz Erbring, *Internet and Society: A Preliminary Report* (Palo Alto, Calif.: Stanford Institute for the Quantitative Study of Society, 2000), chart 10; Neu, Anderson, and Bikson, *Sending Your Government*, 131.

9. Anthony G. Wilhelm, *Democracy in the Digital Age: Challenges to Political Life in Cyberspace* (New York: Routledge, 2000), 50–52.

10. U.S. Department of Commerce, *Falling*, 25–26.

11. U.S. Department of Commerce, *Falling*, 11.

12. Neu, Anderson, and Bikson, *Sending Your Government*, 133.

13. Nie and Erbring, *Internet and Society*, n.p.

14. National Center for Education Statistics, *Digest of Education Statistics* (Washington, D.C.: National Center for Education Statistics, 2000), chap. 2.

15. Linda Ann Riley, Bahram Nassersharif, and John Mullen, *Assessment of Technology Infrastructure in Native Communities* (Washington, D.C.: Economic Development Administration, 2000), 50–52.

16. The Sentencing Project, *Facts about Prisoners and Prisons*, www.sentenc ingproject.org/brief/facts-pp.pdf, 18 Dec. 2000.

17. World Wide Consortium, *Web Accessibility Initiative*, www.w3.org/ WAI/, 19 Dec. 2000.

18. James Madison, "To William T. Barry, August 4, 1822," in *James Madison: Writings*, ed. Jack N. Rakove (New York: The Library of America, 1999), 791.

19. Madison, "To William T. Barry," 791.

20. Victoria J. Rideout, Ulla G. Foehr, Donald F. Roberts, and Moyann Brodie, *Kids & Media @ the New Millennium* (Menlo Park, Calif.: The Henry J. Kaiser Family Foundation, 1999), 11–13.

21. Dan Schiller, *Digital Capitalism: Networking the Global Market System* (Cambridge, Mass.: The MIT Press, 1999), 123–29.

22. Jeffrey Scheuer, *The Sound Bite Society: Television and the American Mind* (New York: Four Walls Eight Windows, 1999), 29–32.

23. Anthony G. Wilhelm, *Closing the Digital Divide: Enhancing Hispanic Participation in the Information Age* (Claremont, Calif.: Tomás Rivera Policy Institute, 1998).

24. Verba, Schlozman, and Brady, *Voice and Equality*, 381–84.

25. Centre for Educational Research and Innovation and the National Center on Adult Literacy, *Schooling for Tomorrow: Learning to Bridge the Digital Divide* (Paris, France: Organisation for Economic Co-operation and Development, 2000), 4.

26. Robert Putnam, *Bowling Alone: The Collapse and Revival of American Community* (New York: Simon & Schuster, 1999), 283–84.

27. Putnam, *Bowling*, 179.

28. Karen Chapple and others, *From Promising Practices to Promising Futures: Job Training in Information Technology for Disadvantaged Adults* (San Francisco: Bay Area Video Coalition, 2000), 2–5.

29. Mitchel Resnick and Natalie Rusk, "Computer Clubhouses in the Inner City: Access Is Not Enough," *The American Prospect* 27 (July-August 1996): 60–68.

30. National Center for Education Statistics, *Teacher Use of Computers and the Internet in Public Schools*, U.S. Department of Education, nces.ed.gov/pubs2000/quarterly/summer/3elem/q3-2.html, 20 Dec. 2000.

31. National Center for Education Statistics, *Internet Access in U.S. Public Schools and Classrooms: 1994–99*, U.S. Department of Education 2000, nces.ed.gov/pubs2000/2000086.pdf, 20 Dec. 2000.

32. National Center for Education Statistics, "Internet Access," 2.

33. Lew Friedland and Harry Boyte, "The New Information Commons: Community Information Partnerships and Civic Change," in *The Center for Democracy and Citizenship*, www.publicwork.org/commons/commons.htm, 20 Dec. 2000.

34. Schiller, *Digital Capitalism*, chap. 3.

35. Lawrence K. Grossman and Newton N. Minow, *A Digital Gift to the Nation: Fulfilling the Promise of the Digital and Internet Age* (New York: Century Foundation, 2001).

36. Advisory Committee on Public Interest Obligations of Digital Television Broadcasters, *Charting the Digital Broadcasting Future* (Washington, D.C.: National Telecommunications and Information Administration, 1998), 24–26.

37. Philip M. Napoli, *Market Conditions and Public Affairs Programming: Implications for Digital Television Policy*, (Washington, D.C.: The Benton Foundation, 2000), 3.

38. Sandra J. Ball-Rokeach and others, "The Challenge of Belonging in the Twenty-First Century: The Case of Los Angeles," Metamorphosis Project 2000, www.metamorph.org/vault/belonging.html, 20 Dec. 2000.

39. Lake Snell Perry and Associates, "Education and Digital Television: Seizing the Opportunity to Realize the Medium's Potential," The Benton Foundation 1999, www.benton.org/Television/edtv.html, 20 Dec. 2000.

The Internet and an Informed Citizenry

9

MICHAEL X. DELLI CARPINI AND SCOTT KEETER

ANEW COMMUNICATIONS environment, driven largely by the Internet and World Wide Web, is rapidly changing the economic, social, and political landscape. According to recent surveys, nearly seven in ten Americans (68 percent) now use computers at least "occasionally," six in ten (59 percent) have computers in their homes, and more than half (55 percent) have access to the Internet, 43 percent of these from home. Of the 55 percent of Americans who are "wired," more than one-third (36 percent), or 20 percent of the general public, now go online five or more hours per week. These numbers are up significantly from just a few years ago. For example, the number of Americans who say they go online at least occasionally has increased from 21 percent in 1996 to 54 percent in 2000.[1]

Although much of this increased Internet traffic is devoted to work, entertainment, and/or personal consumption, the Web has also become an increasingly important source of news (see table 9.1). One-third of Americans (33 percent) report going online for news at least one day per week, nearly one-fourth (23 percent) at least three days per week, and 15 percent every day. Although the Internet is not yet a predominant news source for campaigns—in February 2000, only 7 percent of citizens reported that the Internet was one of their top two sources for campaign news (up from 2 percent in 1996)—nearly one-fourth (24 percent) said they "regularly" or "sometimes" learned something about the presidential campaign or candidates from the Internet.[2]

The civic potential of the Internet is especially strong among younger Americans. For example, one recent survey found that 70 percent of 18- to 25-year-olds believe the Internet is a "useful" source of political and issue information (compared to 48 percent of those

Table 9.1   Patterns of Computer and Internet Use among the U.S. Public

	September 1996	April–May 1998	July 1999	February 2000	April–May 2000
Computer use	56	61	67	67	68
Goes online	23	36	52	52	54
Goes online for news:					
At least once per week	8	20	29	25	33
At least 3–5 days per week	4	13	19	16	23
Every day	1	6	12	9	15
Getting most of your news about the presidential campaign from . . . (1–2) responses accepted):					
Television	75			73	
Newspapers	44			33	
The Internet	2			7	

Source: Surveys conducted by the Pew Research Center for the People and the Press.

over 25), outstripping television news, newspapers, radio, magazines, personal conversations, and direct mail.[3]

As Internet use has increased, newspaper readership and television news viewing has declined. The percentage of Americans reporting that they "regularly" read a daily newspaper fell from 71 percent in 1990 to 63 percent in 2000. Larger declines have occurred in the regular watching of national television news broadcasts (from 60 percent in 1993 to 30 percent in 2000) and local TV news (from 76 percent to 56 percent). Even regular cable news viewing has declined, from as high as 30 percent in 1990 to 21 percent in 2000. Online news sites (CNN.com, ABCNews.com, MSNBC.com, etc.) are consistently rated as more believable than their broadcast or cable equivalents.[4]

Greater Internet use has coincided with increased availability of news and political information on the Web. All of the national broadcast and cable news networks have web sites, as do most local affiliates and major newspapers. Campaign web sites are becoming the norm for national and statewide candidates and are also increasingly common in races for local offices. One would be hard-pressed to find a federal or state government office, or office holder, without a public web site. And the number of both nonpartisan and advocacy groups that have an Internet presence is large and growing.[5]

There is little doubt that the way citizens consume political and public affairs information is changing. Less clear are the implications of this transformation for the practice of democratic politics. Whether the emerging information environment will be little more than "old wine in new bottles," will further erode the already less than optimal state of civic life, or will usher in a new, more participatory citizenry and responsive government remains an open question. In this chapter we explore the potential impact of the Internet on a specific but crucial element of democratic citizenship: political knowledge. In the next section we briefly summarize the current state of political knowledge, making the case for why an informed citizenry is an important requisite for a well-functioning democracy. We then turn to a discussion of the qualities of the Internet that could potentially affect citizens' ability to learn about politics, offering some data to suggest a relationship between Internet use and political knowledge today. Finally, we conclude by speculating on the ways in which the Internet (and its future incarnations) might be used to increase Americans' political knowledge.

What Americans Know about Politics and Why It Matters

Several decades of research provide fairly compelling evidence for five conclusions regarding what Americans know about politics: (1) the average American is poorly informed but not uninformed; (2) average levels of knowledge mask important differences across groups; (3) most citizens tend to be information generalists rather than specialists; (4) knowledge is a demonstrably critical foundation for good citizenship; and (5) little change has occurred in any of these tendencies over the past fifty years.

The American Public Is Underinformed but Not Uninformed

One of the most common conclusions drawn from survey research is that citizens are poorly informed about political institutions and processes, substantive policies, current socioeconomic conditions, and important political actors such as elected officials and political parties.[6] For example, in an assessment of more than 2,000 survey questions[7] tapping factual knowledge of politics, the average level of knowledge was low: more than half of those surveyed could only answer four in ten of these questions. Similarly, in a fifty-question test covering a range of topics designed to tap knowledge of three key areas (institutions and processes, current issues and social conditions, and key political actors and groups), the average score for a national sample of American adults was about 50 percent correct. [8]

Among the questions that less than half of the public could answer were many facts that seem crucial to effective citizenship, including definitions of key terms such as liberal and conservative, knowledge of many rights guaranteed by the Constitution, and where candidates, parties, and public officials stood on important issues of the day. Yet although the public can be characterized as poorly informed, it is not uninformed. Majorities demonstrated knowledge of rudimentary but potentially important facts such as the meaning of the presidential veto, key civil rights such as the constitutional guarantee to a trial by jury, the positions of presidential candidates and political parties on at least some of the major issues of the day, social and economic conditions such as the existence of a budget deficit or surplus, and the like.

Average Levels of Knowledge Mask Important Differences across Groups

Although the mean knowledge level is low, the variance is high: there are dramatic differences in how informed Americans are. For example, on the fifty-question political knowledge test mentioned above, the most informed 30 percent of the sample averaged better than seven in ten correct answers and the least informed 30 percent could only answer one in four questions correctly.[9] In short, there is no single portrait of the American citizen: a substantial percentage is very informed, an equally large percentage is very poorly informed, and the plurality of citizens falls somewhere in between.

One could argue that we should naturally expect "some distribution across people and across issues of the cognitive demands of self-government" and ultimately that civic life must "integrate citizenry competence with specialized expert resources."[10] The problem with this view is that differences in knowledge parallel other, more traditional, indicators of political, social, and economic power. For example, fully three-quarters of women in a 1989 survey had knowledge index scores below the median for men. Substantially more than three-quarters of Americans from families earning less than $20,000 per year scored below the median for those earning more than $50,000, as was the case for post-baby boomers when compared to pre-baby boomers. And three-quarters of black Americans scored below the twenty-fifth percentile of white Americans, a knowledge gap of dramatic proportions.[11] Similar patterns are found in other studies.[12] These group differences reflect the combined consequences of many factors, including systemic differences in educational achievement; social location; employment; motivation to follow politics; and the extent to which efforts are made by political actors to mobilize people to political action.

Citizens Tend to Be Information Generalists Rather than Specialists

One might argue that low and inequitably distributed aggregate levels of political knowledge are not incompatible with the existence of a myriad of distinct "issue publics." This version of the pluralist model of civic engagement posits a population of numerous well, but narrowly, informed issue publics that collectively ensure a healthy democracy. Although there are reasons to suspect that citizens focus their attention on issues of personal concern and so, collectively, would be informed about different aspects of politics, the evidence suggests that to the extent citizens become informed they do so across a wide spectrum of issues and topics.[13]

That most citizens are political generalists rather than specialists is consistent with what researchers know about the information environment and news gathering habits of the public over the past several decades. Most citizens do not read the elite newspapers that provide extensive coverage and so facilitate the acquisition of selective, detailed, in-depth information. Moreover, most television (the premiere source of political information for most citizens) provides relatively homogenized and surface-level information on current politics. As a result, the population is better described as general information haves and have-nots rather than as a collection of selectively informed issue publics.

Knowledge Is Tied to Many Attributes of Good and Effective Citizenship

Evidence of systematic differences in political knowledge, especially when tied to other socioeconomic indicators of political power, should give one pause. The significance of these knowledge gaps depends, however, on whether or not knowledge matters to effective citizenship. Although there is some disagreement on this, our own work and our reading of the larger literature strongly suggests that informed citizens are "better" citizens in a number of ways.

Specifically, research has found that better informed citizens are more accepting of democratic norms such as political tolerance; more politically efficacious; more likely to be interested in, follow, and discuss politics; and more likely to participate in politics in a variety of ways.[14] Research also suggests that informed citizens are more likely to have opinions about the pressing issues of the day,[15] to hold stable opinions over time,[16] and to hold opinions that are ideologically consistent with each other.[17] They are also less likely to change their opinions in the face of new but tangential or misleading information[18] but more likely to change in the face of new relevant or compelling information.[19]

There is also evidence that political knowledge affects the opinions held by different socioeconomic groups (for example, groups based on race, class, gender, and age differences). More-informed citizens within these groups hold opinions that are both significantly different from less-informed citizens with similar demographic characteristics and arguably more consistent with these citizens' material.[20] For example, informed women are more supportive of government programs designed to protect women's rights, informed but economically disadvantaged citizens are more supportive of government programs designed to provide jobs and improve their standard of living, and so forth. These group differences are large enough to suggest that aggregate opinion on a number of political issues would be significantly different and more representative of the public interest were citizens more fully and equitably informed about politics.[21]

Finally, political knowledge increases citizens' ability to consistently connect their policy views to their evaluations of public officials and political parties as well as to their political behavior. For example, more-informed citizens are more likely to identify with a political party, approve of the performance of office holders, and vote for candidates whose policy stands are most consistent with their own views.[22]

Little Change Has Occurred in These Patterns over the Past Fifty Years

Although data allowing for a systematic comparison of knowledge levels over the past 50 years are less comprehensive than one would hope, the evidence strongly suggests that the mean level of knowledge among Americans is about the same today as it was fifty years ago.[23] Similarly, the knowledge gap between men and women, whites and minorities, and rich and poor is no narrower now than it was several decades ago, and there is some evidence that the gap between older and younger Americans has widened.[24]

The lack of change in the mean level of knowledge can be seen as good news or bad news, depending on one's perspective. The good news is that, despite concerns over the quality of education, the decline in newspaper readership, the rise of sound bite journalism, the explosion in national political issues, and the waning commitment to civic engagement, citizens appear *no less* informed about politics today than they were half a century ago. The bad news is that despite an unprecedented expansion in public education, a communications revolution that has shattered national and international boundaries, and the increasing relevance of national and international events and policies to the daily lives of Americans, citizens appear *no more* informed about politics today.

The relative stability in levels of political knowledge should not be mistakenly interpreted as suggesting that Americans are unable to monitor changes in the political environment, however. There are many examples of significant learning by the public. For example, as the Republican and Democratic parties differentiated themselves on the issue of civil rights in the 1960s, public perceptions of their positions tracked the changes. In the early 1960s, the public was divided on which party was more committed to civil rights. By the late 1960s, the public (correctly) perceived the Democrats as more liberal on this issue by a five-to-one margin.[25]

Theorizing about the Internet's Potential Impact on Political Knowledge

Given the stability in aggregate levels of political knowledge over the past half century with such dramatic changes in the information environment, we might expect the introduction of a new form of communications to have little impact on this aspect of citizenship. However, the Internet and other digital technologies are different enough from the past to warrant a closer look.

Although more than ten years old, the work of Abramson, Arterton, and Orren provides a useful summary of what is new about the "new media" environment.[26] Specifically, they identify six core properties: (1) greater volume of available information (and reduced cost of both distributing and receiving information); (2) greater speed in the gathering, retrieving, and transmitting of information; (3) more control by consumers in what they receive; (4) greater ability of senders to target their messages to specific audiences; (5) greater decentralization of the media; and (6) greater interactive capacity.[27] How might these properties affect citizen knowledge? As even a brief exploration suggests, it is not hard to see why theorists are of several minds regarding the likely impact of the Internet.

Below, we explore several scenarios regarding the potential consequences of the Internet for the level, distribution, structure, and use of political knowledge in the United States. Using survey data from several recent studies of the public conducted by the Pew Research Center for the People and the Press, we also offer some initial evidence regarding the plausibility of these scenarios.[28]

Changes in the Aggregate Levels of Knowledge?

The most optimistic scenario is that the Internet will help increase the mean level of knowledge while not exacerbating (and perhaps even reducing) existing gaps in knowledge across socioeconomic groups. This view is based on the assumption that the availability of information is a key determinant in how informed citizens are. Since 1997, 14 trillion megabytes of information have been put on the Internet, with the volume growing daily.[29] This wealth of information provides unparalleled opportunities for citizens to access political information of almost any kind from a variety of sources. In theory, greater volume (and thus opportunity to access information) should translate into a more knowledgeable public.

In addition, it is possible that interest or motivation can more easily be translated into political knowledge in this new information environment. Research suggests that people are more likely to learn about politics if information is available when it is most relevant to them.[30] The Internet goes even further than television in its ability to draw public attention to breaking issues and events (for example, the entire American public had online access to the Independent Counsel's report on the Clinton scandals less than an hour after Clinton himself received it) and does so in a way that combines television's visual and oral cues with the benefits of textual information. Citizens can literally play the role of newspaper editor or news producer, determining what information they receive, how much they receive, and when they receive it. As citizens are more likely to learn about politics when they are interested or motivated, this greater control can mean greater knowledge. And even though most citizens are generalists rather than specialists, interest and learning about a particular aspect of politics could serve as a gateway into the world of politics more generally, eventually leading to a more informed public overall.

Just as the Internet offers greater control to consumers, it also offers producers the ability to gather data on consumers' interests and habits and to use these data to reach large audiences with highly personalized messages. This increases the likelihood that citizens will receive information of interest or relevance, thus furthering the likelihood of political learning. Given the incentive of information producers to reach new and larger audiences, it is also likely that, over time, citizens would be exposed to new messages that are related (but not identical) to topics in which they have already shown an interest, thus slowly expanding their knowledge base. Similarly, greater interactivity and greater decentralization provide opportunities to be exposed to information and points of view that differ from one's own, sparking new interests that in turn can lead to seeking new information.

A second and perhaps equally plausible scenario would predict a general decline in levels of political knowledge, however. In this view the Internet serves to divert the public from things political—a giant box of chocolates that lures citizens away from the nourishing food they need. We know that at least some political learning occurs because citizens are exposed to political information in the course of daily life, even if they do not seek it out. To the extent that the new information environment provides greater opportunities to avoid politics, such passive learning is less likely to occur. In addition, it becomes less likely that citizens will be exposed to the kinds of new information that, by sparking a new interest or piquing one's curiosity, can lead to political learning. The increasing dominance of commercial over civic interests on the Internet may further erode levels of knowledge as politically relevant information becomes increasingly less available relative to nonpolitical information. And Internet-driven declines in the opportunities and need to directly interact with other citizens in public spaces (especially with citizens different from oneself) could further erode the kind of community bonds that lead to political interest and thus to political learning.[31]

Both of these scenarios assume increased penetration of the Web. Although this may be a safe assumption, it is by no means assured, especially in the short run. Although there is a clear upward trend in use of the Internet for news and political information, the percentage of individuals going online has been relatively stable over the past year, as has computer use overall. Technological changes such as increased bandwidth, smaller and more ergonomically comfortable computers, and the convergence of television and the Web may increase the pace of Internet use—but a simple projection from current trends suggests that growth in the population of online users is slowing down.

Regardless of trends in overall use, current data suggest that people who go online for news are better informed than those who do not. Evidence for this can be found in a 1999 survey by the Pew Research Center for the People and the Press. On an eight-point knowledge index (including familiarity with the candidates for the Democratic and Republican presidential nominations), those who reported going online for news every day received an average score of 5.5, while those who never went online averaged 4.2, a difference as large as that found between whites and blacks or between men and women. Other Pew surveys with different measures of knowledge show similar differences between Internet users and nonusers. Internet use remains a significant predictor of political knowledge even when we control for demographic and political differences among users and nonusers.

We cannot conclude from this finding that the Internet *causes* greater knowledge, but it is clear that greater knowledge and extensive use of the Internet for news gathering and greater knowledge go together. Thus, we might assume that the mean level of knowledge for the citizenry as a whole will increase as more citizens use the Internet. But will the benefits be spread across the full spectrum of the public as the Internet achieves greater penetration? The evidence for this is mixed and appears dependent on the interaction between opportunity, motivation, and ability.

Increases in Knowledge Gaps?

Political learning occurs when citizens have the ability, motivation, and opportunity to do it.[32] As noted above, the Internet provides unprecedented opportunities to access information and so should continue to increase overall levels of political knowledge among those who go online. But is opportunity alone enough to increase political knowledge? In the case of traditional mass media (print and electronic), there is at least some evidence to support this. For example, research conducted in Virginia demonstrated very dramatically that residents of the Richmond area (where state politics is regularly covered in the local media) were significantly more informed about state political leaders and issues than were residents of other parts of Virginia where such news was less readily available. The differences were especially large when Richmond was compared to the northern Virginia media market, where the media must divide their coverage of local and state issues across three major jurisdictions (Virginia, Maryland, and the District of Columbia). These differences were demonstrable even after controlling for a broad range of factors known to affect political learning.[33] In short, the information environment affected aggregate levels of knowledge regardless of citizens' interest or ability to learn.

But it is not clear that there is an appropriate analogy between the Richmond and northern Virginia media markets and the comparative opportunities to learn about politics provided by the pre-Internet and current information environments. For example, although it is now quite easy for a resident of northern Virginia to use the Internet to learn what is going on in state government (by looking at the web sites of the Richmond-based *Times-Dispatch* or the Norfolk *Virginian Pilot*, both of which devote considerable attention to state politics), there is little reason to think citizens will be exposed to this information unless they have the motivation and ability to actively seek it out.

Most likely, both passive and active learning occurs with Internet use. If this is correct, we would expect citizens who go online for news to be somewhat more informed than those who do not. But we would also expect online users who are motivated to follow politics (and so more likely to fully exploit the Internet's resources) to learn more than those who are less motivated.[34] That is, we would expect to see an interaction between motivation and going online.

The 1999 Pew Research Center survey provides confirmation of this pattern. Paying more attention to government and politics is associated with significantly higher levels of knowledge about the presidential candidates (both prominent and obscure) and other facts in the news. Similarly, going online for news is associated with higher levels of such knowledge as well (even taking account of demographic differences between those who go online and those who don't). But knowledge levels rise more steeply for Internet users than for nonusers as attention to politics rises (figure 9.1).

Among young citizens—those aged 18–29—the interaction is even stronger (figure 9.2). In fact, the interaction between going online for news and paying attention to politics is the strongest single predictor of political knowledge. As the figure shows, among respondents who follow politics "most of the time," those who go online for news daily score a full point higher (on an eight-point scale) than those who never go online. Indeed, among those who say they pay attention to politics "hardly at all," increased use of the Internet for

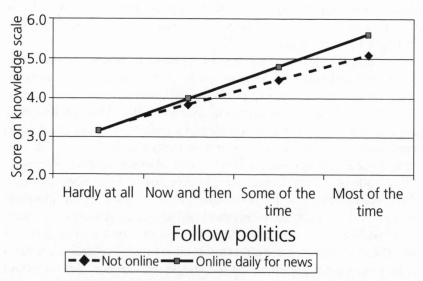

Figure 9.1.   Attention to politics, online news gathering, and political knowledge

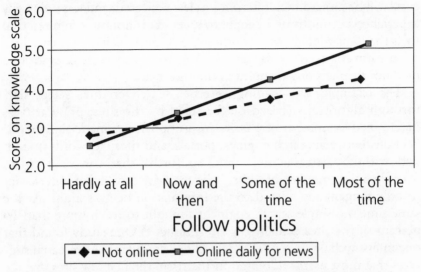

Figure 9.2. Attention to politics, online news gathering, and political knowledge (age 18–29)

news is *negatively* associated with political knowledge. In the absence of motivation, more time spent on the Net—even in the pursuit of news—is associated with holding less knowledge of the type measured here.

This evidence suggests that the Internet, at least in its current form, is an excellent information resource for people who are motivated to gather information about politics. Those individuals are apt to benefit greatly from access to and use of the Internet. To the extent that they learn more about politics, the mean level of knowledge in society will rise. But it is equally clear that although less-motivated individuals may also benefit from use of the Internet, at best these gains will be less dramatic, increasing the gap between information haves and have-nots. The rising tide may not lift all boats equally.

Two additional qualities of the Internet as it is currently configured seem particularly likely to exacerbate this tendency. The first is that although the cost of retrieving information on the Internet is small, the cost (financial and psychological) of entry to the Internet remains nontrivial. The second (and in the long run more important) quality is that with greater volume and fewer gatekeepers come greater costs associated with organizing and finding relevant information, and these costs will be more difficult for poorer, less educated, and less politically experienced or motivated people to meet. This notion, often referred to as the "knowledge gap hypothesis," has been well documented for other forms of mass media[35] and is likely to be especially relevant to a medium as inherently complex as the Internet.

For example, the leading Internet search engines select sites through algorithms (based on fees paid by the sites; popularity as determined by number of visitors; institutional and financial interconnections between search engines, portals, and sites; keywords imbedded within particular sites; and so forth) that can lead to an overwhelming number of "hits," the majority of which are irrelevant or only tangentially related to the information being sought. At the same time, no single search engine is thought to reach more than 16 percent of the sites actually on the Internet.[36] One study found that one in five web pages is twelve days old or younger.[37] As research suggests that most users seldom go further than the first few sites that are called up by search engines, much of the power of the Internet can be lost. Effectively navigating this complex environment can put a premium on interest and ability, exacerbating existing differences in knowledge based on socioeconomic differences. This gap will also be increased by the likely tendency of political information producers (candidates, news outlets, interest groups) to target their messages to those citizens who are most likely to respond.

As is well known, the Internet audience is considerably more affluent and educated than the general public. Figure 9.3 shows the percentage of individuals of different levels of educational achievement who report going online for news at least three days per week. The figure illustrates a very strong association between education and Internet use for news, with those who have some graduate school experience nearly four times as likely to go online for news as those who only finished high school. But the figure also suggests that the association between educational achievement and online news gathering was usually as strong or stronger in 2000 as it was a year earlier. The pattern for income, race, and gender is similar: The gaps in Internet use for news between rich and poor, black and white, and men and women are as large now as a year ago. Indeed, a statistical analysis that takes account of many different demographic influences on online news gathering in 2000 (using age, income, education, race, and gender) produces virtually identical results in nearly every respect

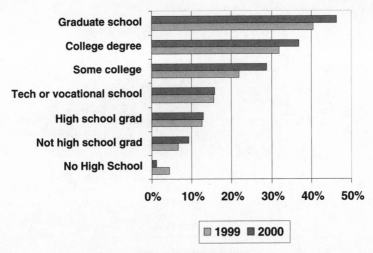

Figure 9.3.   Online for news at least 3 days per week

to the same model using 1999 data. If socioeconomic characteristics were becoming less critical in affecting who surfs the Internet for news, we would expect to see these characteristics' importance in such a model decline between 1999 and 2000, but this does not occur.

One comparison between 1999 and 2000 goes against the grain of our other findings, however. Figure 9.4 shows the percentage of respondents of different ages who report going online for news at least three days during the past week. (Each data point in this graph is an average of results from individuals covering a five-year age span. For example, the entry for 30-year-old respondents averages data from respondents who are 28, 29, 30, 31, and 32 years old. This technique is called a five-year moving average and helps to smooth out fluctuations in the trend line that result from sampling error and other random sources.) At least two conclusions are readily obvious. First is that in both years of the survey, younger individuals were more likely to report going online for news than were older respondents. The second is that although increases between 1999 and 2000 can be seen for most age groups, the greatest growth in online news gathering is among citizens under age 35.

Figure 9.5 shows the age-related trend for regular use of newspapers and television news in 1998 and 2000. The pattern is just the opposite. Older citizens are much more likely to use these media, and

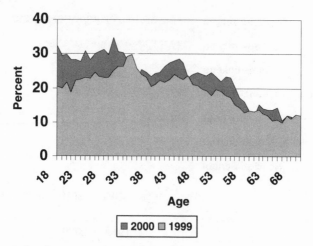

Figure 9.4.   Online for news at least 3 days per week

the younger citizens evidence a larger falloff in use between 1998 and 2000. Taken in combination, figures 9.4 and 9.5 suggest that the pattern of news consumption for younger Americans is changing dramatically, but the growth of online news use may not be a harbinger of greater political awareness among younger cohorts: online news use

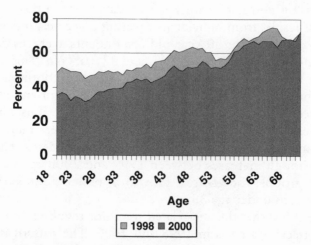

Figure 9.5.   Regular use of newspapers and TV news

may simply make up for what is lost in the use of more traditional media.[38]

We do not have adequate data to examine possible changes in the "knowledge gap" over time, but taking account of growing Internet use, we did examine the gap in 1999, comparing those who gather news on the Internet with those who do not. In comparisons of men and women, blacks and nonblacks, and younger and older citizens on the knowledge index described earlier, we found the knowledge gap to be no narrower among those who used the Internet for news than those who did not. This was true whether or not we controlled for other demographic characteristics such as education, income, and attention to politics.

The Growth of Information Specialists?

A third possible impact of the new information environment is to discourage the kind of information generalist quality that currently characterizes informed citizens. The Internet's greater volume coupled with greater consumer control, targeting, and decentralization will allow citizens to focus on the specific levels of politics (e.g., local, national, international) and substantive issues (e.g., abortion, the environment, the economy) in which they are most interested. Once chosen, producers of information are likely to give these consumers more and more of the same, creating very different information environments for different segments of the public. The deliberative, interactive aspects of the Internet will only serve to reinforce this fragmentation as citizens self-select or are exposed to only those chat groups or other venues that are frequented by like-minded people. Gary Selnow suggests that this fragmentation carries dangers for a political system that is otherwise built on a consensus of views among a popular majority of voters. One such danger is that citizens will miss issues that occur outside of their particular surveillance patterns. The second is that citizens will "run the risk of an information blind spot within an issue when they chase down sites given to partisan and ideological viewpoints."[39]

But increased specialization may not inevitably be bad for the system if the specialized knowledge gains are in addition to a continued pattern of general surveillance. Moreover, to the extent that the Internet helps previously uninvolved citizens develop an interest in specific issues, this could serve as a gateway to more general political interest (and thus general political knowledge) as they come to feel more connected to the system and more politically efficacious.

We are much too early in the life of the Internet to say with any certainty where the path ahead is leading. But some preliminary indicators are suggestive of trends. A Pew Research Center survey conducted in 2000 asked respondents which is more important: "getting news that gives you general information about important events that are happening, or getting news that is mostly about your interests and what's important to you." Two-thirds (67 percent) of respondents preferred general news, but 28 percent wanted information relevant to their personal interests. Figure 9.6 shows the relation between this question and going online for news. As the chart indicates, heavy Internet news consumers are only slightly less likely to want general news—at least for now. And though younger respondents were a little more likely than others to want news of specific relevance to them, there was no clear pattern of increased interest in personalized news among the heaviest users of the Internet in this age group.

The other datum of relevance to this question pertains to the potential displacement of other media by the Internet. If Internet users are less likely to read newspapers or watch television news, the

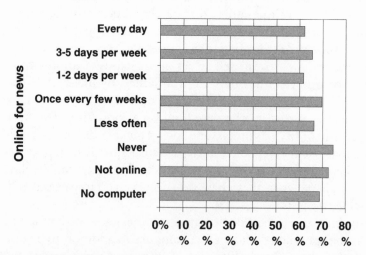

Figure 9.6.   Prefer news that gives general information about important events rather than news about your interests

agenda-broadening benefits of those media may wane. The 2000 Pew survey asked online news seekers if they were using other sources of news more or less often than before (only those going online for news at least one to two days per week were asked this question). Overall, 58 percent said there was no change in their use of other media, but 10 percent said they were using other media more often, and 18 percent reported using other media less often, with television and newspapers accounting for most of the loss. But, as might be expected, displacement was most likely to occur among those who go online the most. Among those who gather news every day on the Internet, 28 percent said they were using other sources less often.[40]

The Consequences of Political Knowledge: The Marriage of Information and Action?

A final consideration is how the Internet might affect the relationship between political knowledge and citizenship. Political knowledge and political action are strongly linked in the literature on participation, and so any impact of the Internet on levels of political knowledge of the sort discussed above should translate into changes in the amount and type of participation. In addition, however, the Internet has the potential to affect the strength of the link between information and action either by easing the ability to participate or, in contrast, by providing opportunities for pseudopolitical activities that have no impact on the political process.

It is unclear whether the Internet, as presently configured, will promote conventional forms of political participation. Bimber's analysis of 1996 and 1998 National Election Study data on participation suggest that the only demonstrable linkage thus far is between Internet use and financial contributions to campaigns in 1998.[41] We may reasonably guess that this connection has been strengthened since 1998, if for no other reason than that contributions via the Web were illegal in that election cycle.

Despite the apparent lack of impact to date, the Internet's most unique characteristics—the marriage of increased information, targeting by providers, filtering and active self-selection by consumers, and bidirectionality of communication—seem to offer truly new prospects for civic engagement. In particular, the Internet's ability to provide information to a citizen and simultaneously permit him or her to act on that information (e.g., by communicating a reaction to friends, interest groups, or public officials; giving money; signing a petition; registering and voting; joining an organization; agreeing to attend a meeting; etc.) is a radically new feature of the information environment.

Although the Internet's value for increasing civic engagement has only begun to be exploited, there is suggestive, if anecdotal, evidence of its potential. For example, it appears that the Internet was critical to organizers of the Seattle protests against the World Trade Organization, to the anti-land mine campaign, and to the Free Tibet movement. Bimber provides two additional examples of mobilization via the Internet: a national campaign on homeschooling and a local issue involving the homeless in Santa Monica, California.[42] He describes this general phenomenon as "accelerated pluralism," arguing that the Internet will not change the basic logic of pluralism. Citizens will continue to participate in politics and be mobilized largely through groups to which they belong. At the same time, Bimber writes, the Internet "will lower the obstacles to grassroots mobilization and organization by political entrepreneurs, activists, and others, and will speed the flow of politics. Lower costs of organizing collective action offered by the Net will be particularly beneficial for one type of group: those outside the boundaries of traditional private and public institutions, those not rooted in businesses, professional or occupational memberships, or the constituencies of existing government agencies and programs."[43] He speculates that this, in turn, will lead to an intensification of group-centered politics and a decreased "dependence on stable public and private institutions."

The Longer Term

One of the first newspaper accounts of the (then still experimental) medium of television declared that it was a passing fad that would hold little interest for most Americans and have little long-term impact. Given the poor quality of television's sound, image, and content at that time, it is not hard to see why an observer might draw this conclusion. In many ways the Internet of today is analogous to that flickering image of more than a half century ago, and predictions about its impact are just as likely to fail the test of time.

Nonetheless, the preliminary evidence, subject to many caveats, is that the Internet is already having an impact on the political knowledge levels of citizens who actively use the medium to gather information. This impact is strongest among citizens who are most motivated and able, raising the possibility of (but in no way ensuring) growing divides between information haves and have-nots. There is little evidence to suggest an increasingly fragmented citizenry divided into distinct "information publics." Evidence that the Internet will increase civic engagement is also sparse, though specific examples of its value in mobilizing small but intense segments of the public is suggestive of its potential in this regard.

But it is far too early to know if these partial findings represent a passing stage in the Internet's political development or the beginnings of what will become stronger and more lasting trends. What is clear is that the Internet itself will change. Undoubtedly there will be a convergence between television (and other media) and the Internet. Miniaturization of hardware, growing sophistication of software, and increased bandwidth into the home carry with them several implications. First, it will be ergonomically much easier to spend time on the Internet than it currently is. Citizens will be able to get the full functionality of the Internet from their couches or easy chairs, with the television serving as a computer monitor and a television simultaneously. Small, comfortable, book-like devices will bring the functionality of television and the Internet to the lap. Thus, one important disincentive to Internet use will be removed. Second, convergence means that whatever we call news will increasingly combine the qualities of television, newspapers, and the Web. News shows undoubtedly will continue to be created with many of the same production values they have today. But newscasts, like virtually all other programming, will be available on demand and can be stopped and started at the convenience of the viewer. Many viewers will still want to watch an entire newscast, but a menu will be available (as with today's DVD movies) from which stories can be chosen. These systems will also provide the kind of text-based resources we currently enjoy on the Web. Searching for information will get easier and be more likely to return what the seeker is looking for.

These changes will mean that citizens can dig deeper if they choose to do so and that it will take fewer cognitive resources to be successful in a search; it will also mean that citizens can avoid news more readily than in the present. The political impact of these changes will continue to depend on the ability and motivation of citizens, coupled with the radically transformed opportunities to learn and to translate this knowledge into action. In turn, this ability, motivation, and opportunity will depend as much as on the content and context of this new information environment as on the technology itself. And as always, this is ultimately a question of political choice, power, and imagination.

Notes

The authors are also grateful to the Pew Research Center for the People and Press, which provided several national surveys used in the chapter. Authorship is equal; names are listed alphabetically.

1. Pew Research Center for the People and the Press, *Investors Now Go Online for Quotes, Advice: Internet Sapping Broadcast News Audience*, Washington, D.C.: 11 June 2000a; Stanford Institute for the Quantitative Study of Society, *Study Offers Early Look at How Internet is Changing Daily Life*, www.stanford.edu/group/siqss/Press_Release/press_release.html, 2000.

2. Pew Research Center for the People and the Press, *Education and Maintaining Prosperity Are Top 2000 Priorities, Gore Gains, Bradley Looks More Liberal*, Washington, D.C.: 19 January 2000b.

3. Project Vote Smart, *Project Vote Smart National Survey on Youth and Civic Engagement,*. www.vote-smart.org/index.phtml, 14 September 1999.

4. Pew Research Center, *Investors Now Go Online for Quotes.*

5. A review of state government web sites can be found at www.digital govt.com/statesprogram.html.

6. Stephen Earl Bennett, "Know-Nothings Revisited: The Meaning of Political Ignorance Today," *Social Science Quarterly* 69 (1988): 476–90; Angus Campbell, Philip E. Converse, Warren E. Miller, and Donald E. Stokes, *The American Voter* (New York: John Wiley and Sons, 1960); Philip E. Converse, "The Nature of Belief Systems in Mass Publics," in *Ideology and Discontent*, ed. David E. Apter (New York: Free Press, 1964); and Russell W. Newman, *The Paradox of Mass Politics: Knowledge and Opinion in the American Electorate* (Cambridge, Mass.: Harvard University Press, 1986).

7. These questions covered a range of topics one might expect an informed citizen to know, including knowledge of institutions and processes (for example, how a bill becomes a law, or what rights are guaranteed by the U.S. Constitution), of substantive issues and indicators of the day (for example, whether there is a federal budget deficit or surplus, or the percentage of Americans living in poverty), and of public figures and political organizations (for example, the name of your U.S. Representative, the stands of presidential candidates on the key issues of the day, or which party controls the Senate).

8. See also Michael X. Delli Carpini and Scott Keeter, *What Americans Know about Politics and Why It Matters* (New Haven, Conn.: Yale University Press, 1996).

9. Delli Carpini and Keeter, *What Americans Know about Politics*.

10. Michael Schudson, *The Good Citizen: A History of American Civic Life* (New York: Free Press, 1998), 310, 311–12.

11. Delli Carpini and Keeter, *What Americans Know about Politics*, 161.

12. The one exception was race, in which the knowledge gap was less dramatic than in the 1989 survey (approximately three-quarters of blacks scored below the median for whites). We attribute the smaller knowledge gap to the predominance of party-oriented questions in the 1988 survey.

13. See Delli Carpini and Keeter, *What Americans Know about Politics;* and John Zaller, "Analysis of Information Items in the 1985 NES Pilot Study," report to the Board of Overseers for the National Election Studies, 1986.
We acknowledge that our understanding of this aspect of political knowledge is limited by practical difficulties in gathering data about the depth of knowledge people have regarding very specific issues. Research by Shanto Iyengar ("Whither Political Information," Report to the Board of Overseers and Pilot Study Committee, National Election Studies, 1986) is suggestive of the possibility that issue specialists exist, and we agree that there are many citizens with special expertise on topics such as social security, tax policy, environment issues, and the like. We suspect, however, that such issue "experts" would also have a reasonably strong base of knowledge about general political topics.

14. Delli Carpini and Keeter, *What Americans Know about Politics;* Jane Junn, "Participation and Political Knowledge," in *Political Participation and American Democracy*, ed. William Crotty (New York: Greenwood Press, 1991); Jan Leighley, "Participation as a Stimulus of Political Conceptualization," *Journal of Politics* 53, no. 1(1991): 198–211; George E. Marcus, John L. Sullivan, Elizabeth Theiss-Morse, and Sandra L. Wood, *With Malice toward Some: How People Make Civil Liberties Judgments*, (New York: Cambridge University Press, 1995); Sidney Verba, Kay L. Schlozman, and Henry R. Brady, *Voice and Equality: Civic Voluntarism in American Politics* (Cambridge, Mass.: Harvard University Press, 1995).

15. Delli Carpini and Keeter, *What Americans Know about Politics;* Jon A. Krosnick and Michael A. Milburn, "Psychological Determinants of Political Opinionation," *Social Cognition* 8, no. 1 (1990): 49–72.

16. Delli Carpini and Keeter, *What Americans Know about Politics;* Robert S. Erikson and Kathleen Knight, "Ideological Sophistication and the Stability of Ideological and Partisan Sentiment," paper presented at the annual meeting of the American Political Science Association, Washington, D.C., 2–5 September 1993; Stanley Feldman, "Measuring Issue Preferences: The Problem of Response Instability," *Political Analysis* 1(1989): 25–60.

17. Converse, "The Nature of Belief Systems in Mass Publics," in *Ideology and Discontent*, ed. Apter; Delli Carpini and Keeter, *What Americans Know*

152   MICHAEL X. DELLI CARPINI AND SCOTT KEETER

about Politics, 235–38; Herbert McClosky, and John Zaller, *The American Ethos: Public Attitudes Towards Capitalism and Democracy* (Cambridge, Mass.: Harvard University Press, 1984), 250–51; Neuman, *Mass Politics,* 64–67; Norman H. Nie, Sidney Verba, and John R. Petrocik, *The Changing American Voter* (Cambridge, Mass.: Harvard University Press, 1979), 154; James A. Stimson, "Belief Systems: Constraint, Complexity and the 1972 Election," *American Journal of Political Science* 19 (1975): 393–417; Zaller, "Analysis of Information Items," 10–11.

18. Donald R. Kinder and Lynn M. Sanders, "Mimicking Political Debate with Survey Questions: The Case of White Opinion on Affirmative Action for Blacks," *Social Cognition* 8, no. 1 (1990): 73–103; David J. Lanoue, "One that Made a Difference: Cognitive Consistency, Political Knowledge, and the 1980 Presidential Debate," *Public Opinion Quarterly* 56 (summer 1992): 168–84.

19. John R. Zaller, *The Nature and Origins of Mass Opinion* (New York: Cambridge University Press, 1992).

20. Delli Carpini and Keeter, *What Americans Know about Politics,* 238–51. In some cases greater information also seems to lead "more advantaged" citizens (e.g., whites) to hold opinions that are more supportive of government policies designed to assist the less advantaged (e.g., minorities).

21. Scott L. Althaus, "Information Effects in Collective Preferences," *American Political Science Review* 92 (1998): 535–58; Delli Carpini and Keeter, *What Americans Know about Politics.*

22. R. Michael Alvarez, *Information and Elections* (Ann Arbor: University of Michigan Press, 1997); Delli Carpini and Keeter, *What Americans Know about Politics,* 251–58.

23. Bennett, "Know-Nothings Revisited;" Delli Carpini and Keeter, *What Americans Know about Politics,* 105–34; Neuman, *Mass Politics,* 14–17; Eric R.A.N. Smith, *The Unchanging American Voter* (Berkeley: University of California Press, 1989), 159–222.

24. Delli Carpini and Keeter, *What Americans Know about Politics.*

25. James A. Stimson, "A Macro Theory of Information Flow," in *Information and Democratic Processes,* ed. James Kuklinski and John Ferejohn, 345–68 (Urbana: University of Illinois Press, 1990) 352–53.

26. Jeffrey B. Abramson, F. Christopher Arterton, and Gary R. Orren, *The Electronic Commonwealth: The Impact of New Media Technologies on Democratic Politics* (New York: Basic Books, 1988), 32–65.

27. Also see Neuman's propositional inventory of the characteristics of the new media ("New Media, Public Knowledge And Political Behavior." Paper presented at the annual meeting of the American Political Science Association, Atlanta, Georgia, Sept. 2–5, 1999).

28. Measuring the effects of the mass media on characteristics of the public such as political knowledge is difficult. One problem is that with many media—especially television—exposure is so widespread that comparisons of the exposed and unexposed are hard to make. This is not yet a challenge with research on the

Internet, as nearly half of the public remains unexposed to the Internet. A more difficult problem is ascertaining the direction of causality. If people in an audience are better informed than those not in the audience, does this mean that they learned from the medium, or did the well-informed choose to attend to the medium because of greater interest in the subject or awareness that the medium was a good source? In the end, both dynamics are likely to be at play. At a minimum, correlations (controlling for possibly confounding demographic and attitudinal factors) between levels of knowledge and media use are highly suggestive of the potential informational value of those media.

29. Institute of Governmental Studies, " E-Campaigning: The Internet Revolution Comes to Politics," www.igs.berkeley.edu:8880/publications/par/May2000/index.html, May 2000.

30. Delli Carpini and Keeter, *What Americans Know about Politics.*

31. Robert Putnam, *Bowling Alone: The Collapse and Revival of American Community* (New York: Simon and Schuster, 2000).

32. Robert C. Luskin,"Explaining Political Sophistication," *Political Behavior* 12 (1990): 331–61.

33. Delli Carpini and Keeter, *What Americans Know about Politics,* 209–17.

34. Neuman, 1999.

35. P. J. Tichenor, G. A. Donohue, and C. N. Olien, "Mass Media Flow and Differential Growth in Knowledge," *Public Opinion Quarterly* 34 (1970): 159–70.

36. Steve Lawrence and Lee Giles, "Accessibility and Distribution of Information on the Web," *Nature* 400(1999): 107–9.

37. John Markoff, "As Web Expands, Search Engines Puff to Keep Up," *New York Times* (29 May 2000): 3C.

38. In 1998, 49 percent of the youngest age group (18–29) used neither the Internet nor the two traditional sources of news (newspapers and television) on a regular basis. In 2000, the comparable figure was 48 percent. Thus, the rise of news gathering on the Internet has displaced news gathering from other sources; in any event, the total percentage attending to the news (from any of these major sources) has not increased.

39. Gary W. Selnow, *Electronic Whistle-Stops: The Impact of the Internet on American Politics* (Westport, Conn.: Praeger, 1998), 193–94.

40. The impact of this is unclear, as web sites operated by the major television networks and newspapers are the most popular. Thus, simply moving from one medium to another does not mean that the content viewed will be entirely different.

41. Bruce Bimber, "Information and Political Engagement in America: The Search for Effects of Information Technology at the Individual Level," *Political Research Quarterly* 54: 1 (March 2001).

42. Bimber, "The Internet and Political Transformation: Populism, Community, and Accelerated Pluralism," *Polity* 31 (1998): 133–60.

43. Bimber, "Information and Political Engagement in America."

The Internet, Democracy, and the Future

IV

E-Democracy: Lessons from Minnesota

STEVEN CLIFT

E-Government by Day, E-Citizen by Night

IN THE FALL OF 1993, I found myself staffing a task force on electronic access to government information for the state of Minnesota. The next spring, the task force's studies resulted in the large, citizen-oriented Minnesota Government Information Access Council, to which I was appointed. As a part of my work on the council, I coordinated North Star, the state home page and portal to Minnesota government. Around the same time as all this, I was among a number of citizen volunteers who came together to create the world's first election-oriented web site, called Minnesota E-Democracy. Thus, for three years I explored two new worlds: I ran one of the best-known web sites in Minnesota during the day and pursued my dream of helping to build an interactive citizenry through Minnesota E-Democracy at night.

Today, there are thousands of important democracy online accomplishments around the world. However, transforming democracy through the use of the Internet has scarcely begun. I am not interested in simply adapting democracy "as is" to the Internet. Now that the e-commerce hype wave is passing, there is a returning interest in the civic ideals of the Internet. In this chapter, I hope to point out some of the exciting contributions and possibilities that will help us as Americans to build an Internet that contributes to the future of democracy and to its purpose. We in this country need to shift our attention from election-oriented online politics toward meaningful e-governance and e-citizen activities. During the next few decades, we can change democracy for the better and develop "wired" ways that enable people to improve their lives and the world around them. In our local communities and regions, in our nation, and around the world we are at the beginning of an era we ourselves can define.

The fundamental question we must ask ourselves is "As democracy and the Internet converge, how must we be involved now to improve both?" The challenge for us, as citizens, is to be engaged in this process of change. The primary sources of online political information today are government, the media and dot-com content providers, candidates and political parties, and advocacy groups. The private sector and others in the information technology industry are developing information and communication tools and standards that will fundamentally influence this arena. Based on who is doing what, we need to ask the question "What is missing?"

A partial answer begins with the Internet's capacity for people to organize and communicate in groups. It is within the context of electronic free assembly and association that citizens will gain new opportunities for participation and a voice in politics, governance, and society. We can be engaged through existing institutions, be they nonprofits, universities, the media, companies, or governments. We can also be involved as individual citizens through the creation of new organizations that are *of* the Internet, not just *on* it.

As with the founding of any modern nation, the choices made today, the ideals upheld, the rules adopted, and the expectations created will determine the opportunities for democratic engagement for generations to come.

Government Online—Representative E-Governance and Democracy

Government is an important user of the Internet. Parliaments, legislatures, and local councils are making meeting agendas and minutes, bills, reports, and existing laws available online. Elected officials, whether heads of government or local councilors, are sharing more and more information online that can bring them closer to their constituents. In considering these uses with respect to democracy, let's set aside the politics of technology or the role of government as an Internet regulator or law enforcer. Too often, the "hands off" ethos related to government regulation of the Internet inhibits the building of public support for the resources necessary to help improve online government service delivery, provide citizen access to government information, and fundamentally open up Internet-enhanced representative decision-making processes.

It is important to point out that a schism exists between the administrative side of government, which controls most public-sector IT (information technology) resources, and government decision-making bodies that represent the people. Improved service delivery must not be disconnected from the two-way democratic potential of the Internet. We do not want governments to simply automate services without a public evaluation of what they are doing. Governments must undertake fundamental reviews and interactive approaches if they are to develop the legitimacy that will be required to govern in the information age. They need to meet the expectations citizens will increasingly develop as they become consumers of commercial web sites and users of e-mail in their everyday lives.

The online public already wants quick and efficient government online services from an accessible and well-organized public portal. The online medium allows it. The users of this new medium demand it. Beyond that, however, a "Democracy Button" should exist on all government sites. From there, citizens should be able to find explanations of government and agency processes and find out how they can affect those processes. Democracy requires citizen understanding of government responsibilities and functions, including funding sources and levels.

Moving Representatives and Public Decision Making Online

The first area in which we must advance online government for democracy is in representative and decision-making bodies and processes. The best way to enhance online citizen involvement in decision making is to incorporate online tools into the official democratic processes. We must make a substantial investment to upgrade the information infrastructure of parliaments, legislatures, local councils, commissions, and task forces at all levels of government. We need systematic full access to legally public information. We need to create opportunities for citizen participation at each step and at every locale where official decisions are made. The current pattern consists of one-way advocacy to government, punctuated by protests; this raises the noise level of democracy while not adding to the quality of democratic deliberations.

Take the current use of e-mail, for example. E-mail is clogging the in-boxes of elected officials, who are slow to adopt tools to sort it, filter it, and respond to it electronically.[1] This situation makes e-mail the least effective channel for an average citizen to influence government. On the other hand, e-mail is an extremely effective tool for insiders who try to correspond with officials and staff they know. Reforming this situation could begin with an e-mail response system based on open source software (i.e., software that can be developed publicly). Officials as well as citizens would have much to gain from such a scenario. If approached strategically, online public input into the government can improve the decision-making process and actually reduce the total administrative load of constituent contact.

Government decision-making bodies should have online operations that allow any citizen to search public information databases in advanced ways (pull) and to receive automated notification (push) of meeting notices and proposals of interest. Citizens could indicate interest in a certain topic area or a specific law and then be notified whenever changes to that law are proposed. There should be open standards-based public directory databases with contact information for all bodies and for their elected and appointed officials. There should be a legal requirement to announce all public meetings online. Public meetings should have live and archived audio or video streams available whenever recording is legally required. The development of searchable digital archives of key decision-making documents for historical purposes should also be integrated into these systems.

Governments have a special duty to ensure broad access to formal participatory processes. Decision-making bodies should host well-organized online interactive hearings and events to complement their in-person public hearings. Citizens should be able to testify live via the Internet to public officials and audiences. If three public hearings are held around a region on a certain topic, the fourth one should be online. That way, participatory opportunities will be available to all, regardless of where they live, how readily they can travel, and indeed their knowledge of or access to the Internet.

How do your local governments measure up? Although you cannot do all these things at once, a government of the people will only take on the functions and responsibilities that people ask for and make a priority. Here are a few shining examples:

- *Online input into formal decision making:* The Central Bucks School District redistricting plan www.cbsd.org/redistricting/ in Pennsylvania received more than 500 comments via e-mail—the vast majority of all comments received. The chair of the school board felt that the online feedback helped the board evaluate where changes were required. Concerns were raised about the lack of public access to the comments received and about how quickly the in-person public hearing went.

    Another good example of a government welcoming online public input involves the new Scottish Parliament, working with the International Teledemocracy Center www.teledemocracy .org. The Parliament has agreed to accept official public petitions via the Internet. The system was used by the World Wildlife Fund to garner 305 signatures in support of marine parks as part of a national park system for Scotland.[2] Unlike third-party petition sites, this is a formal petition recognized by the Parliament.
- *Online government consultations:* In the Netherlands, an ongoing discussion with Minister Roger van Boxtel (www.rogervan boxtel.nl/), facilitated by the Instituut voor Publiek en Politiek (Dutch Centre for Civic Education), builds on extensive Dutch experience with online consultations. The Centre established a clear response mechanism and time frame to ensure prompt replies to citizen comments and questions.[3] The key was guaranteed facilitator access to the Minister to develop responses on controversial issues. Many online government consultations place civil service staff in the difficult position of speaking publicly, perhaps politically, for their agency, but at a minimum, staff need prior permission to share existing agency policy and provide factual information.

    There is nothing worse than an online consultation in which citizens wonder if anyone is listening and in which no government response is forthcoming. This lesson was learned with discussion forums on U.K. Prime Minister Tony Blair's web site (www.number-10.gov.uk), leading to dramatically better practice with their Policy Forum on Electronic Delivery of Government Services. The forum asks users to read a discussion document and then to add comments to the online discussion; official posts and responses from staff are clearly marked.

Governments in the United States are not leaders in this area. The Smart Growth forum of the Metropolitan Council (www.metrocouncil.org) in Minnesota is one of the few official government-run and -sponsored online discussion spaces.

▪ *Online parliamentary consultations:* The Hansard Society for Parliamentary Government (www.hansard.org.uk), the educational wing of the U.K. Parliament, has hosted a series of invited expert interactive forums at (www.democracyforum.org.uk) in conjunction with committees in both the House of Lords and the House of Commons. At the request of a parliamentary committee, an invited group discusses a topic, from which a high-level report is generated. Topics covered thus far include electronic democracy, women in science, and domestic violence.

Led by two U.S. senators, the "E-Government: An Experiment in Interactive Legislation" effort (cct.georgetown.edu/development/eGov/) will hopefully lead to a future in which similar types of applications to those in the U.K. will run on the official web sites of U.S. legislatures. In the state of Minnesota, the role of the Internet in Jesse Ventura's election as governor in 1998 prompted the state Senate Democrats to host the first open citizen discussion forum on an official state or national legislative web site. The next step is to integrate the interactive capabilities of the Internet into the official committee hearing process.

▪ *Official government exploration:* In late 1999, the state of Victoria in Australia (www.mmv.vic.gov.au) announced the first government-sponsored "Democracy Online" initiative, with the goal of finding "how best to use new technologies to open up the processes of Parliament and government to the people of Victoria."[4] All governments should begin to formally ask themselves questions about their official use of the Internet, including funding requirements and possible law changes that will enhance official representative democracy in the information age. It is important to point out that providing election access to decision-making information and processes requires resources. Representative bodies at all levels have squeezed out about as much as they can of existing IT and communications budgets for their rudimentary online public services.[5]

A Civic Web Agenda

Although government initiatives in online democracy are to be wel-
comed, citizens should not wait for them to arise. Many questions
need independent deliberation in civil society. For instance, to what
extent should a democratic information system serve the interests of
those who govern, versus those who want to influence how they are
governed? Should the government link citizens—that is, help those
petitioners who indicate interest in the same topics or proposals to
become aware of each other? With personalization comes the potential
abuse of data about peoples' political interests and behaviors; how
should these data be protected? How will the Internet public-access
infrastructure in libraries, schools, and other locations be part of a
Democracy Information Infrastructure (DII) that includes training
and assistance? (See chapter 8 for more on this.) If a government cannot afford to build a DII on its own, what models can be developed
to promote the sharing of tools and costs among governments as well
as to promote connections to the commercial Internet?

Some answers will emerge through experience. At Minnesota E-
Democracy, we discovered by accident that election-related activity,
although vitally important, diverts serious attention and energy away
from the use of the Internet in governance. When the 1994 election
was over, the online public commons of Minnesota E-Democracy
(www.e-democracy.org/mn-politics) continued to hum with citizen
dialogue about the issues that mattered to them. This digital dialogue
included public issues before the state legislature and matters of local
politics. Averaging 400 to 500 direct e-mail subscribers to the time of
this writing, the commons, also known as the MN-POLITICS E-Mail
Discussion Forum, quickly became a part of everyday public life in
Minnesota. Its agenda-setting role became well known as more and
more political activists and journalists came online and into the forum.

The lesson our organization learned: Use elections to draw more
people into sustained use of the Internet in democracy. Election activities are launch pads of attention that need to have their energy cap-
tured, not dissipated. The low cost of keeping online forums open
makes this feasible as never before. What goes up during campaign
season need not come down after Election Day. This lesson has rarely
been learned by others.

Another lesson: good discussions foster exchanges between those who *do* politics and those who *talk* politics. The low cost of keeping online forums open makes this feasible as never before. Talkers keep doers on their toes, and doers help focus talkers. Few "average" citizens will waste their time expressing opinions if they feel that no one who can do something about it is listening. Few officials will listen unless they know who is speaking. Minnesota E-Democracy has core rules and guidelines to keep both factions engaged; its two most important rules are a limit of two posts per day per person and the requirement that all posts be signed with the name and city of the author. (On the plusses and minuses of anonymity, see chapter 1.)

In 1998, phase two of Minnesota E-Democracy emerged. We updated our charter, rules, and guidelines for MN-POLITICS and divided the forum into two lists—one for discussion, and one for announcements. More importantly, we took our online public commons model more local: the Minneapolis Issues Forum may just be the most active and dynamic online community issue discussion space in the world. We are building additional forums in more Minnesota cities and are developing extensive outreach proposals to extend the diversity of voices in the forums.

Along with announcement sharing and opt-in discussions, an online commons should have a shared link directory to key resources, a participant directory, and a calendar for related in-person and online events sponsored by the many participating organizations. These interactive spaces need to be managed and promoted in an unbiased manner, such that they can become an important communications crossroads where developing public policies are improved and civic participation is broadened. Web links to government, media, and non-profit web sites will be essential. Through open standards-based syndication, forum content can be excerpted and imported by such other sites.

Civic forums should be augmented with online "practice" sites, where those involved with solving public problems could trade ideas, experiences, and advice on implementation. Examples include peer-to-peer exchanges for those promoting recycling programs and efforts to combat graffiti in their communities. In some cases, implementation could actually occur online, as well. The Internet could facilitate coordination of civic programs and projects.

Conclusion

The next few years are absolutely vital in terms of establishing the expectation that the Internet is and can be used for public purposes. To make the case that noncommercial applications are essential, I argue for a "radical incrementalist" approach. Ask yourself what two or three simple but important things you can do to incrementally contribute to democracy online. Quit waiting for the pie in the sky plan to be finished, or for the big grant to get awarded. In the public square, as in the private sector, the Internet will advance our lives based on trial and error. Whether you are an individual e-citizen or directly involved in advocacy, media, or electoral campaigns, we each need to do our part.

As the role of the Internet in democratic politics evolves, we must ask this question: What public goals can we achieve through the Internet that require us to work in different ways? It seems clear that adapting existing institutions—public, private, or nonprofit—will not suffice. We need to create "Public Internet" partnerships and new mediating institutions. We need a balance of activities and must prevent excessive "dot-com-munism" from limiting "dot-org-anizing" for public "dot-gov-ernance." We need to reflect on what we have learned and envision our public goals ten and fifty years down the road and ask what we must do now to create e-citizens and best serve the public goals of the Information Age.

Notes

1. See *E-Mail Overload in Congress: Managing A Communications Crisis,* Congress Online Project, 19 March 2001, www.congressonlineproject.org.
2. See www.teledemocracy.org/news/ccis-press.htm.
3. See www.publiek-politiek.nl.
4. See www.go.vic.gov.au/research/electronicdemocracy/voting.htm.
5. See www.go.vic.gov.au/research/electronicdemocracy/voting.htm.

The Internet and Dreams of Democratic Renewal

11

LANGDON WINNER

A PERSISTENT, COLORFUL THEME in American political thought is the conviction that new technologies will revitalize democratic society, enabling citizens to command the political and economic resources needed to become effectively self-governing. Sentiments of this kind have reappeared in every generation since the early nineteenth century, a standard motif in the nation's public rhetoric. The building of canals, railroads, factories, and electrical power plants as well as the introduction of the telegraph, telephone, automobile, radio, and television have all been accompanied by enthusiastic proclamations that the innovation would give ordinary folks greater access to resources, more power over key decisions, and broader opportunities for political involvement. With the arrival of personal computers and the Internet in the late twentieth century, this enduring vision has been powerfully rekindled. Many observers have predicted that democracy of a radical kind—decentralizing, antihierarchical, and directly participatory—will surely flow from the widespread use of digital electronics. How well grounded are these expectations of political renewal?

Historical Echoes

Belief in the connection between technology and democracy surrounded the major engineering works of the United States' early years. The Erie Canal, for example, was heralded not merely as a channel carrying freight east and west, but also as the very apotheosis of the common citizen. At the canal's opening in 1825, the *Utica Sentinel* declared that the project was especially notable for "proof which it will present to all mankind of the capabilities of a free people, whose energies, undirected by absolute authority, have accomplished, with a sum insufficient to support regal pomp for a single year, a work of greater public utility, than the congregated forces of Kings have effected since the foundations of the earth."[1] The date chosen for the ritual opening of the canal, as for the start of building or the grand openings of many important technology projects of the period—the Pennsylvania Grand Railroad (1826), the Baltimore and Ohio Railroad (1828), the Baltimore and Ohio Canal (1828), the Boston and Worcester Railroad (1835), and others—was Independence Day. Celebrations of new technical systems on the Fourth of July linked them indelibly to the country's emerging democratic traditions.

The strong association between technical progress and the vitality of citizenship continued through the century. A business magazine in 1841 praised "steam navigation" and other inventions for the way they elevated the political abilities of ordinary folks. "In exact proportion to the extension of political freedom and the diffusion of popular intelligence, has been the advance of invention and the useful arts. . . . As political power has been diffused among the great mass of men, the human mind has been directed to those inventions that were calculated to confer solid benefits upon the mass."[2] Acclaim for technological progress during this period commonly emphasized its contributions to political equality, civic competence, and widening horizons of democratic participation. In 1836, George S. White, a staunch proponent of industrialism, praised the ongoing technical improvements as "a moral machine which, in proportion as it facilitates a constant and rapid communication between all parts of our land, tends most effectually to perfect the civilization, and elevate the moral character of its people."[3]

Through the decades, technical admiration has shifted from one new device or system to the next. Early in the twentieth century, for example, expectations that we today associate with computers and the Internet were strongly attached to the radio. In 1924, Herbert Hoover, then Secretary of Commerce, praised radio for its political potential: "Let us not forget that the value of this great system does not lie primarily in its extent or even in its efficiency. . . . For the first time in human history we have available to us the ability to communicate simultaneously with millions of our fellow men, to furnish entertainment, instruction, widening vision of national problems and national events."[4] For some enthusiasts of radio in that period, the immediacy of radio broadcasts was a harbinger of citizen involvement in politics, marked by stronger links between the public and elected officials. In a 1924 issue of the magazine *Radio Broadcast,* columnist Mark Sullivan asked, "Will Radio Make the People the Government?" and answered with a wholehearted "yes." "At present," he wrote, "the public is now dependent on the vicarious censorship of the newspaper reporter. . . . The fundamental merit of the radio in Congress will be that it will enable the public to get its information direct."[5]

Encomiums of this kind were not limited to communications devices. The airplane, automobile, plastics, consumer appliances, and massive dams and water systems were widely praised as manifestations of an expanding, populist spirit.[6] Thus, David E. Lilienthal, chairman of the Tennessee Valley Authority, took pains to insist that the TVA—a massive complex of some fifty dams, power plants, and flood control waterways begun in 1933—would not produce obnoxious concentrations of power or centralized control. His book, *TVA: Democracy on the March,* argued that the system was a grand, populist encounter of ordinary Americans with the forces of nature. "When the principles of grass-roots democracy are followed," he wrote, "electricity, like soil minerals, provides men with a stimulus in their own lives, as well as an opportunity to work together with others toward a purpose bigger than any individual. By that act of joint effort, of citizen participation, the individual's essential freedom is strengthened and his satisfactions increased."[7]

Proclamations of civic revitalization through technological innovation have an element of truth. Clearly, the cumulative advances in industrial production, transportation, and communications have improved the quality of life for ordinary citizens. It is reasonable to conclude that through the development of electronic communication devices, people are better educated and better informed about the social and political world. Americans have taken advantage of the instruments of production and communication available to them to advance their personal and group interests. A great many technologies now comprise key elements within the fabric of American political society; indeed, it is scarcely possible to imagine modern democracy without its panoply of technical devices.

During the past two centuries, however, the rhetoric praising the latest marriage of technology and democracy has also tended to ignore some salient facts, overlooking broader patterns of sociotechnical development, including ones that cast a shadow on hopes for greater equality, participation, and effective democratic citizenship. Thus, although the railroads were praised as transportation that would help democratize the United States and make the continent more accessible to a mass populace, by the latter decades of the nineteenth century the railroads became the focus of populist protests by farmers and small-town folks who saw their destinies controlled by centralized banks and railroad lines. In similar ways, early expectations that the factory system would become a jewel in the crown of the republic were soon overshadowed by decades of labor struggles over wages, hours, benefits, and, more broadly, over conditions on the assembly line. Though the factory did contribute to improvement in the lives of working people, it was also widely regarded as a place of regimentation, inequality, and oppressive social relations.

By the same token, the democratic romance of the automobile (still very much with us) must also be seen within the setting of a larger social and political drama. During the twentieth century's middle decades, the construction of superhighways and ring roads produced an escape route through which mainly white, middle-class suburbanites abandoned the industrial cities and left behind the less well-to-do groups. Taken within the whole system of land use, mortgage subsidies, and transit planning, the automobile became the linchpin of economic, social, and political divisions that vex American democracy to this day.

In short, hopes for political equality, inclusion, shared power, and wider participation cultivated by increasing use of instrumental systems are bedeviled by a host of problems. Ecstatic visions of "technodemocracy" have historically fallen short in their unwillingness to acknowledge the complex social, organizational, and political circumstances in which the technologies were situated. But the recurrence of technology-related malformations and disorders has never quelled the dreams of renewal. As each new technical device or system has burst onto the scene, all previous histories and troubles were simply forgotten, replaced by renewed confidence that society had at last stumbled upon something wonderful and without precedent.

Hope Reborn

During the late twentieth century, the penchant for locating political salvation in the realm of instruments shifted to electronic and digital technology. As computer communications spread from military and corporate organizations into society, advocates proclaimed that citizens were being showered with a wonderful gift, a tool that would restore the power of self-government to everyday people. Predictions of this kind were central to Alvin Toffler's 1981 bestseller *The Third Wave*, in which computers and the "electronic cottage" were upheld as the wellspring of a new political populism.[8] Writings during the 1980s on the information society gave optimistic projections of the unfolding of "the computer revolution," especially the radically democratizing effects of the personal computer. Now ordinary folks would have computing power to rival that of the largest organizations.[9]

By the early 1990s, however, the focus of political hopes shifted from the personal computer (PC) to computer networks and their potential for empowering citizens. One of the earliest and best known statements of promise was Howard Rheingold's *The Virtual Community* (1993). Careful to present his utopia as an appealing possibility rather than a necessary future, Rheingold's views echoed the classic hopes for technology and politics of earlier generations. "The political significance of [computer mediated communication] lies in its capacity to challenge the existing political hierarchy's monopoly on powerful communications media, and perhaps thus revitalize citizen-based democracy." Based on his observations of Internet chat rooms, Rheingold predicted that a "citizen-centered, citizen-controlled worldwide communications network," an "electronic agora," was at hand.[10]

At the end of the decade, such hopes were still very much alive and were still announced as if they were a totally new breakthrough. Thus, Andrew Shapiro in *The Control Revolution* laments that the evolution of modern, liberal representative democracy has left the key political choices in the hands of elected public officials. "Now, though," he argues, "technology may allow us to make many of these choices for ourselves. We could become not just citizens, but *citizen-governors*—each of us playing a role in governing the distribution of resources, the wielding of state power, and the protection of rights."[11]

Expressions of this kind have become the coin of the realm in journalistic portrayals of the Internet, as they have in hundreds of online chat rooms. The experience of many computer users leads them to believe that the world is being rapidly democratized by the spread of networked computing, and that their own influence over decisions has expanded. Feelings of empowerment through personal involvement in cyberspace are now energetic and widespread.

Perhaps the good news is that the predicted revitalization of the public sphere via the Internet will doubtless amplify dozens of earlier techno-democratic revolutions, the very ones that already should have made the American polity a utopia renowned for its ideal conditions of economic equality, broadly dispersed power over decisions, soaring levels of political participation, and unprecedented traditions of direct citizen empowerment. Nevertheless, faced with happy projections of success, one must still pause to ask some serious questions. Is a democratic revolution taking place? Is there, for example, a leveling of political influence, a diminishing concentration of economic and political power in the hands of the few? What are we to make of the claims that the Internet helps generate a new, vital, and effective form of democracy?

By now it is clear that the Internet is a highly popular new medium. Americans seem eager to jump on board, use e-mail, enter chat rooms, and browse the billions of pages on the World Wide Web. Surveys by National Public Radio and the UCLA Center for Communication Policy indicate that roughly two-thirds of adults in the United States use the Internet, at least on occasion.[12] Although there are still significant inequalities in access to the Internet, these differences appear to be narrowing as computer use becomes a fixture of everyday life at all economic levels.

Surveys of Internet users also indicate that for those able to log on, there are often strong feelings of exhilaration in the use of e-mail and Web browsers, in having access to vast sources of information, news, and entertainment as well as opportunities to talk with people and to extend one's sphere of contacts. A common impression seems to be that we have overcome the confines of electronic communications that long characterized the broadcast media. One is no longer subject to messages transmitted from one source or a very few sources. At one's fingertips is a virtually unlimited universe of information providers. For this reason, many people who use the medium experience a sense of liberation, noticing that to some extent they can control the kinds of connections they have to news and information, including sources that are not filtered (or at least less filtered) by the editors, news programmers, and other arbiters of "acceptable" information.

In the same vein, many people enjoy organizational relationships that seem less encumbered by hierarchy, free of the authorities and social structures that formerly served as intermediaries within the flow of information, goods, and services. Many enthusiasts of the Internet believe that the elimination of organizational layers within innovative, global business firms will now inevitably extend to political relationships as a whole. In his widely read *A Declaration of the Independence of Cyberspace*, John Perry Barlow informs the "governments of the Industrial World" of their pending irrelevance: "I declare the global social space we are building to be naturally independent of the tyrannies you seek to impose on us. You have no moral right to rule us nor do you possess any methods of enforcement we have true reason to fear."[13]

Equally important for many Internet enthusiasts is the possibility that ordinary people will become producers, not merely consumers, of widely disseminated electronic information. Because anyone can write messages, create Web pages, start newsletters, initiate contacts, and organize online interest groups, the possibilities for expressive, deliberative citizenship seem bright. In this regard, the attractions of the online world sometimes become positively seductive. Recently, feminist scholar Ellen Balka looked back on tendencies in feminist thinking about technology and society. She noted that during the past decade or so, there has been a distinct decline in the frequency and quality of feminist contributions to that debate. "Where," she asks, "have all the feminist information technology critics gone? We've gone online everywhere the technology has been available to do so, and in our enthusiasm for the technology, have lost that critical feminist perspective." In Balka's view, involvement with the Internet is rapidly replacing other kinds of direct, face-to-face political engagement.[14]

Looking to the realm of conventional politics—election campaigns, the activities of lobbyists, attempts to shape public opinion—it is clear that the Internet is now a means to mobilize political interests quickly and easily. As illustrated throughout this book, groups and individuals from across the ideological spectrum are using web pages, listservs, and electronic mail to organize and publicize their points of view. The global character of the Web makes this all the more appealing because it not only offers the prospect of a wider dissemination of one's message, but also makes this more difficult for any outside agency to control. For instance, neo-Nazi and other racist groups subject to legal restrictions in Germany at present are moving their web sites to computer servers in the United States, thus avoiding police power over their propaganda. Although the worldwide, digital flow of political ideas has raised hopes of greater understanding and respect among different racial groups, there is no guarantee this will occur.

Again, as this book has shown, election campaigns at all levels now typically have one or more web sites that present the views of candidates. One arguably new feature is that opponents of a candidate and his or her views can produce inexpensive and appealing satires that at first seem real. During the 2000 presidential campaign both George W. Bush and Albert Gore were buffeted by web sites that carried their names and photos, offering fictitious, comic news releases and policy statements. The site www.GWBush.com, for example, advocated a general presidential amnesty for persons still jailed for the youthful indiscretion of possessing drugs.[15] The rapidly increasing use of the Internet as a conduit for jokes is one of the more surprising developments in recent years. Whether this can be counted as a positive contribution to public discourse or just another expression of citizen bile remains unclear.

One can offer endless examples to support the conclusion that the Internet is making important contributions to democracy. But how should we weigh these claims within a broader understanding of today's politics?

Reality Checks

There can be little doubt that the Internet has already become an important feature in contemporary political culture. Networked computing offers an opportunity for lively and diverse means of expression. In this respect it strongly resembles other domains of popular culture—entertainment, sports, fashion, and consumerism among the more important—that have played a democratizing role in modern society. Consumer goods, for example, have become a means through which people express themselves; what they buy, what they wear, what they possess and use can symbolize their lives. The market responds to these expressions of popular tastes, desires, and preferred identities by trying to produce more of them through advertising. Hollywood films and television programs, similarly, reflect a democratic culture by providing a mirror for the fantasies of mass audiences. A substantial portion of the organization and content of Internet communication at present can be placed squarely in the same category, a contribution to a culture of widely shared but highly commercialized symbols, messages, and meanings.

But do these *cultural* manifestations of democracy also qualify as a genuine contribution to democracy in a more basic *political* sense? Is the mobilization of people's attention and activity on the Internet effective when it comes to matters of power and policy? Does networked computing improve the quantity and quality of citizen participation?

Asking questions of this kind, one recognizes that the Internet— like technologies heralded in the past—cannot be seen as an entity that exists by itself, something isolated from other political practices and organizations. Enthusiasts of Internet democracy often make arguments along the following lines. "On one side we observe the dominant patterns of politics as usual, the politics of statecraft, political parties, and so forth that used to be the focus of power. On the other side, the Internet side, there are wholly new patterns of computer networks in which hierarchies have vanished, where power is up for grabs, where new expressions of citizenship are in the making." Such arguments seem appealing until we notice that, of course, the two political realms clearly occupy the same political space. If the activities of online communication do not substantially modify patterns of influence over key decisions, making such influence more broadly shared than before, then announcements of a democratic revolution are at best premature.

Of course, developments in the longer term cannot be anticipated with any great confidence. The interpenetration of Internet and political society is still in process, with the outcomes highly uncertain. Who knows what our politics will look like in another twenty years? But one can take note of patterns that exist today that suggest that continuity, not rupture, is characteristic of the influence of online structures and practices upon politics and configurations of social power.

Take voter turnout, for example. The Internet seems to have had little effect so far upon the numbers of people who actually go to the polls. (For recent data, see chapter 4.) In the United States, turnout is usually 50 percent or less.[16] Factoring in the people who do not register to vote, this means that roughly 25 percent of the populace becomes an effective plurality, a governing force. Swing voters in many elections—typically middle class men and women, concerned with tax rates, education, and social security—constitute an even smaller slice of the populace, and receive a disproportionate share of candidates' attention. These trends in American elections are worrisome and are occasion for a great deal of cynicism. They generate a mood of embittered contempt for politics that skillful politicians manipulate to their advantage. So far, the Internet has done nothing to alter either nonvoting or political exploitation of itself.

What of the suggestion that people are finding new arenas for public discussion and citizen activity on the Internet, arenas focused on particular interests, issues and campaigns? There is something to be said for this interpretation, exemplified in chapter 10. However, in sheer volume of participation, there does not seem to be an increase during the era of the Internet as compared to the era of television or the newspaper. Indeed, Robert Putnam's studies of civic culture show a steadily declining involvement of citizens in public life since World War II.[17] The numbers of people who are willing to engage in citizen activities beyond paying their taxes and obeying the laws is dwindling. Yes, there remains a highly visible and vocal minority that now finds the Internet a godsend. But if democracy means anything, it means widespread involvement of ordinary people in matters of governance. The participation trend does not seem especially hopeful, unless one takes widespread torpor as a sign that people basically are contented.[18]

What of the idea (again, see chapter 10) that democracy is experiencing a revival, given the energy of political discussion, debate, and information gathering? The early reports are also not especially promising. The ideal of democratic discourse as seen in the ancient polis, seen in the New England town meeting, and celebrated in the writings of John Dewey and Jurgen Habermas, suggests that people with different commitments and points of view should come together to discuss, argue, deliberate, and ultimately decide on a course of action. In truly democratic settings it is the diversity of participants, as well as their commitment to engage persons whose ideas differ from their own, that holds the promise of good government at the end of the day.

Alas, as Galston observes in chapter 3, open and diverse forums are not characteristic of participation on the Internet. People typically "customize" the sources of information that interests them, selecting, for example, only news stories on a particular business interest or their favorite sports team. The Internet makes possible far greater selectivity than old-fashioned newspapers allowed; the press in earlier decades routinely presented readers with a fairly wide range of topics because the editors had to appeal to a broad range of potential readers. Today, users can limit that array of stories to focus on just what concerns them at a particular moment.

The same selectivity can be found in Internet chat groups and list-servs. Like-minded people share information and ideas, reinforcing opinions they held in the first place. On the Internet, as in face-to-face political settings, people are often uncomfortable with ambiguity, disagreement, and expressions of diverse points of view. In face-to-face meetings, however, there is sometimes a moment in which people feel the need to come together and seek compromise. Indeed, this is one of the great prizes of political communication in democracy: a desire to speak one's mind, to listen to other points of view, and then to seek common ground. Unfortunately, many of today's online forums lack this quality. Most of the time, one finds people of similar viewpoints talking to each other. When diverse voices and viewpoints do emerge, it is often with a criticism and harshness that is characteristic in some online discussions. People stay around long enough to deliver a few shots and then vanish, a luxury that the Internet allows. By comparison, geographically situated communities tend to make such critics more accountable for their words; one has to get up the next day and face one's neighbors. So far, the Internet seems far better for venting and flaming than for seeking democratic solutions.

Political scientists would not be surprised to see that deliberative discussions are not taking shape online. Numerous studies point out that increasing the amount of information or the number of channels of communication available to citizens does nothing to improve either the willingness to participate in politics or the quality of participation when it occurs.[19] The idea that having access to vast resources of electronically packaged information will make people more knowledgeable, effective citizens does not always test true. Something else must happen within the space of communication if active, deliberative democracy is to come to life.

That extra element, in my view, involves direct, sustained engagement with others in communities of concern to each individual about issues that affect his or her life. For many decades the political party system in America satisfied this condition to some extent, although in ways that were not fully democratic. Ordinary people would bring a concern to the local political party boss, who organized forces for the party and who paid some attention to the needs of people in his ward. The boss would bring those needs to party leaders at higher levels and in legislatures who would then work out the deals that provided at least partial response to the ordinary person's concerns.

In this light, the Internet closely resembles television in that it serves as a replacement for direct contact between ordinary citizens and political leaders, contact of a sort formerly manifest in ordinary party politics. Although the Internet is to some extent more interactive than television in politics, the two share a strong tendency to disconnect the daily lives and immediate needs of everyday folks from the political process. Most citizens lack immediate contact with those who are directly involved in politics or governance. The vast majority of citizens are simply not engaged in the substance of important public issues of the day; neither do they speak with persons who are.

What this means is that the Internet has done little so far to affect the fundamental ways that society is governed. Patterns of deeply entrenched economic power that have long been prominent in what are ostensibly democratic states are still prominent and effective. Elites based in the corporate and financial sectors strongly influence the choice of candidates, shape the ideas of political parties, finance electoral campaigns, and ultimately control the outcomes of government policy making. The continuing lack of citizen engagement is the underlying condition that allows the contemporary exercise of oligarchic power to flourish, leaving democracy as a set of increasingly hollow slogans.

Communications for Whom?

An important question that will confront democratic politics in the coming decades is whether or not the kinds of communication available on the Internet will become (as enthusiasts suggest) an alternative to patterns that now link the electronic media to concentrations of political power, a condition that badly weakens contemporary democracy. The worldwide growth of oligopolies in publishing and the electronic media severely limit the variety of information, news, and public expression available in the newspapers, magazines, books, movies, and television programs that most people encounter.[20] As corporate giants move their operations onto the Internet, offering attractive packages of mass media diversion, the cherished experience of the Internet as a place of unfettered free expression could well be eclipsed. The domain of networked computing and wireless communications has been targeted as the next great marketplace, an enterprise zone the global corporations expect to dominate.

There is now, for example, an enormous push to channel people's Internet browsing through portals, web sites that organize the chaotic range of information on the Internet into orderly, highly commercialized paths in much the same way that cable and satellite television structure television channels. Not surprisingly, many of the Internet portals are owned and controlled by the business firms that also dominate American television. To an increasing extent, the portals convey the impression that the Internet is all about entertainment, sports, shopping, auctions, vacation planning, and other varieties of consumerism. They are notable for their almost total lack of categories and links, which would encourage ordinary Web surfers to explore even the most conventional of political issues. The same underlying sensibility informs cable and satellite channels devoted to the Internet— Tech TV, for example—whose twenty-four-hour-per-day offerings stress digital communications as a pumped-up addition to existing opportunities to shop, play video games, and generally spend money. Contrary to the expectations of Internet visionaries, none of the programs on these "tech" channels feature opportunities for citizen engagement with public issues. Instead, they suggest that the couch potato and mouse potato are close relatives.

Up to this point, attempts to shape the Internet within this corporatized model have not been entirely successful. One can hope that the sheer number and diversity of possibilities for communication on the Internet will favor democratic populism in the end. But Time-Warner/AOL, Yahoo!, the Rupert Murdoch media empire, Disney/ABC, MSNBC, and other global firms are hard at work shaping the flow of electronic information and the profits that will result from this new medium. Scripting the ideas, expectations, and preferences that float through the minds of both politicians and citizens within this domain is a crucial part of what amounts to a well-organized program of social and political manipulation. Well-focused resistance to such influence seems far less evident.

A closely related problem for democracy involves the flagrant corruption in politics and government as candidates and public officials scramble to raise funds for television campaign ads. Because the current trends point to a merger of Internet and television in the not-too-distant future, it seems likely that lamentable fundraising practices will simply be transferred to the new media in cyberspace. Networked computing could easily become a means by which wealthy individuals and organizations buy access and clout, setting the agenda for policies that affect how people live. To this point, enthusiasts for Internet democracy have not owned up to these possibilities, especially the intense commercialization of cyberspace and the likely transfer of existing political pathologies into this new medium. They prefer the familiar, threadbare Utopia fantasies that have endlessly reappeared in American history, fantasies about technology and democracy that have proven a very poor guide for action in the past. To indulge in these utopian reveries while ignoring important political choices—basic telecommunications polices decided in the mid-1990s, for example—is mistakenly called "being optimistic about the future."

Conclusion

Seen as a matter of political communications in general, the crucial issues here have less to do with the peculiarities of any particular medium than with the control of communication channels of all kinds, especially how the rules governing communication access, exclusion, and use are established. In the United States, it has been common practice to develop means of communications in ways that at first seem well connected to broader notions of the public good, but later end up serving private economic interests by and large. The nation typically provides vast amounts of tax money for research and development on electronic media, expecting that the populace as a whole will benefit. But in a pattern repeated for many decades, the government soon divests its stake in the matter, delivering the new communications media into the hands of commercial, profit-seeking enterprises. Through the decades, those who make public policy have been willing to relinquish the public's stake in the airways (and now the Internet) because, it is believed, the corporate sector knows best how to build and manage society's communications facilities.

The folly of giving away the enormous public wealth of electronic resources is bad enough. But these ills are compounded by the effects this policy has in limiting possibilities for common access to new

media in the arts, education, and public affairs. Hence, it is hardly surprising to find that society, which has for many years systematically
shackled the ability of citizens to use the tools of electronic speech
directly, should wake up to find itself with a shriveled, distorted public
sphere and an increasingly cynical populace. The utopian recipe—
"add Internet and stir"—is not likely to change this situation.

A key question, then, is whether our society has the will and commitment needed to set aside a broad cultural domain, one in which
the influence of advertising and of other market forces is limited and
in which the activities of civic culture are nurtured. A consensus for
preserving public, electronic space of that kind, never very strong in
the United States, has all but vanished during the Reagan/Bush and
Clinton eras, as the global market has been embraced as the sole arbi-
ter of social priorities. The Internet as we see it today exhibits this tendency extremely well. What we are witnessing is not the revitalization
of democratic politics but the creation of a vast new sphere for the
development of commercial enterprise.

As headlines on the newspapers' business pages make clear, the
Internet is rapidly moving to a new stage. Television, as it has existed
for the past half century, is giving way to a hybrid of high-definition
television, computer networking, and a host of competing digital formats. The enormous media conglomerates know exactly what they
want from this transformation: unprecedented profits from the dereg-
ulated sphere that combines local and long distance telephone, cable
television, and lucrative Internet services. But what, if anything, will
the citizens of democratic societies demand from the new digital
media? What will they want other than more bandwidth, more sports,
more movies, and a wider range of opportunities for shopping? That
enormously important question awaits widespread attention, study,
and debate.

Notes

1. "The Grand Canal Celebration," *Utica Sentinel*, 8 November 1824,
quoted in David E. Nye, *American Technological Sublime* (Cambridge, Mass.:
MIT Press, 1994), 36.

2. "American Steam Navigation," *Hunt's Merchant Magazine*, February
1841, p. 14, quoted in Nye, p. 38.

3. George S. White, *Memoir of Samuel Slater, Philadelphia, 1836*, reprinted

in *The New England Mill Village, 1790–1860*, ed. G. Kulik, et al. (Cambridge, Mass.: MIT Press, 1982), 355.

4. Quoted in Todd Lapin, "Deja Vu All Over Again," *Wired* 3.05, February 1995, 175.

5. Quoted in Lapin, p. 218.

6. See, for example, Joseph Corn, *The Winged Gospel: America's Romance with Aviation, 1900–1950* (New York: Oxford University Press, 1983).

7. David E. Lilienthal, *TVA: Democracy on the March*, twentieth anniversary ed. (New York: Harper & Row Publishers, 1953), 91.

8. Alvin Toffler, *The Third Wave* (New York: Morrow, 1980).

9. See my discussion of this period in "Mythinformation," in my book *The Whale and the Reactor: A Search for Limits in an Age of High Technology* (Chicago: University of Chicago Press, 1986), 98–117.

10. Howard Rheingold, *The Virtual Community: Homesteading on the Electronic Frontier* (Reading, Mass.: Addison-Wesley, 1993), 14.

11. Andrew Shapiro, *The Control Revolution: How the Internet Is Putting Individuals in Charge and Changing the World We Know* (New York: Public Affairs, 1999), 154.

12. NPR, Kaiser Foundation, and Kennedy School of Government, *Technology Survey*, //npr.org/programs/specials/poll/technology/, issued February 2000; UCLA Center for Communication Policy, *Surveying the Digital Future: The UCLA Internet Report*, www.ccp.ucla.edu, November 2000.

13. John Perry Barlow, *A Declaration of the Independence of Cyberspace*, www.eff.org/pub/Publications/John_Perry_Barlow/barlow_0296.declaration, 9 February 1996.

14. Ellen Balka, "Where Have All the Feminist Technology Critics Gone?" *Loka Alert* 6:6 (11 Nov. 1999), www.loka.org/alerts/loka.6.6.txt.

15. See the web site www.GWBush.com.

16. A recent analysis of this situation is given in Mark Lawrence Kornbluh, *Why America Stopped Voting: The Decline of Democracy and the Emergence of Modern American Politics* (New York: New York University Press, 2000).

17. Robert D. Putnam, *Bowling Alone: The Collapse and Revival of American Community* (New York: Simon and Schuster, 2000). In an earlier article, Putnam searches through several possible causes for the decline of community involvement during the last half of the twentieth century. He writes, "I have discovered only one suspect against whom circumstantial evidence can be mounted, and in this case it turns out, some directly incriminating evidence has also turned up. . . . The culprit is television." See "Tuning In, Tuning Out: The Strange Disappearance of Social Capital in America," *PS: Political Science & Politics*, vol. xxviii, no. 4, December 1995, 677.

18. For an interesting discussion see Nina Eliasoph, *Avoiding Politics: How Americans Produce Apathy in Everyday Life* (New York: Cambridge University Press, 1998).

19. See, for example, Sidney Verba and Norman Nie, *Participation in*

America: Political Democracy and Social Equality (New York: Harper and Row, 1972) and Philip E. Converse, "Change in the American Electorate," in *The Human Meaning of Social Change*, ed. Angus Campbell and Philip Converse (New York: Sage, 1972): 263–337.

20. Robert W. McChesney, *Rich Media, Poor Democracy: Communication Politics in Dubious Times* (Urbana, Ill.: University of Illinois Press, 1999).

The Politics of a Network World: A Speculation   12

MICHAEL VLAHOS

THE POLITICS OF A network world will be the politics of a network civilization, defined by the nature of civic identity and political relationships.

But what is a network world? How is it different from a world with a network? Today's network, after all, is just a geographic grid that exchanges electron packets from one physical terminus to another. How will this electronic architecture encourage the formation of a civilization?

What follows is a set of change postulates. Think of them as possibilities, inasmuch as they are not realities—yet. And how long is "yet"? Like the British imperials who liked to arrange the world to the East of them as Near, Middle, and Far, Americans like to arrange the future into near, middle, and long. Prudent projections always dwell on the near term, with a few safe blandishments tossed out to the middle. Those who risk the long term must content themselves with the light-applause authority of the entertainer, for they will be judged not on what they say, but on how pleasingly they say it. American culture is a culture of the bottom line, and it greatly rewards near-term calls that elevate that line. So the long term tags along just for fun.

Clearly this excursion is headed for the long term. All I can promise is that I will try to entertain a bit in getting there. But there are some serious reasons for risking an argument with merely the brittle authority of the long term. One reason is that The Change—the rise of a network civilization—will not just happen, and it will certainly not happen quickly. Other big changes, such as the crisis period at the end of antiquity or such as the Industrial Revolution, unfolded through generations. For example, parts of the United States were busy industrializing in 1820, but eighty years later the United States was still a nation half-steeped in agriculture.

Great change takes time. Great changes that do emerge very quickly are nevertheless not accepted immediately. As a change begins, people in their maturity tend to reject and deny it. People in their youth try to adapt to it, and children grow up with it simply as normal life. *And the generation after theirs has no living link to the world before the change.* Dramatic civilization change takes four generations. We are in the first generation only. If this excursion stopped at the midterm—say ten years hence—it would be like stopping the industrial chronicle in 1850, or the end of antiquity in 435.[1] However risky, the long term cannot be shirked here.

So these change postulates must hew to a long-term timeline.

The Network Is Everywhere

When will the network be everywhere? When there are a billion network terminals? When there are a billion users? When multi-Mpbs bandwidth is the standard, and T1-level wireless is available everywhere?[2]

Wrong questions. *When* isn't as interesting as *how* this inescapable architecture of human connection will change our way of life. We especially need to see the near-term practical consequences of an encompassing world network.

We can see today how economic activity is migrating to the network. As business-to-business and commercial services rapidly move there, we can see practical consequences in incredibly efficient business relationships and transactions. But it won't stop there. The migration of the world economy to the network is simply the first visible historical aspect of an emerging network world. The existential postulate of change must go deeper: *Because the network is everywhere, everyone can be together. And because all knowledge is in the network, everyone can find the people they want to be with.*

And this—perhaps indirectly at first—begins to point the way to true political transformation, and to the civic basis of network civilization. What does it mean to say "everyone can be together"?

It's Not the Network; It's What You Do with It

By looking at the responses of earlier societies to technology changes, we can see that societies responded differently to essentially the same set of new capabilities. The emergence of a network world itself does not predicate what comes next, any more than the industrial world directed us to specific social and cultural outcomes. In fact, how cultures adapted to industrial capability reveals a broad range of human variation and response.

An example: In the 1950s, the rise of the Interstate highway system led quickly to the rise of national fast food chains like McDonald's. Why? Because people wanted a consistent dining experience on the road. The impact of the Interstate-triggered boost to the car culture on American food habits also perversely intertwined with the impact of the emerging television culture and the new ubiquity of refrigerators. The TV dinner worked together with fast food to essentially destroy American cuisine.[3] But the Japanese—who treasure cars and television every bit as much as we do—never compromised their culinary traditions.

It can be argued that industrialism, in the end and in aggregate, permitted a fairly narrow range of human responses. Successful industrial societies have a lot in common, and what differentiates them at last is the discreteness of culture: the variations we see revealed in unique traditions that cultures strive to retain. Nations live in different places, and as each national culture industrialized, each tried to preserve its own "mystic chords of memory" by embedding cultural identity into the new structures of industrial life. Adapting to industrialism was often a straightforward, if horrendously complex, process of preserving cultural continuity. But in some places continuity was broken. Russia and China both suffered a loss of continuity in ethos. Now, at the very end of the industrial age, both are coming to terms with inner identities ravaged by that particular form of industrializing we call Communism.

So we have some recent historical benchmarks for cultural change in the wake of technology change. Industrial technology changed the structures of social life. Yet the world network encourages much deeper change even than that. It introduces two powerful new dimensions to change: it erases the physical distance between people and it empowers individual persons.

If two existential truths define today's world—the world with a network—they are: (1) the hierarchies and relationships that constitute an international order rooted in terrestrial polities; and (2) the subdivision of individual identity and belonging according to the cultural and political claims of these polities on people. Terminating these truths will unleash our movement to network civilization.

The Network Is Not the Network

To most people today, the network is its hardware: its servers, fiber optic cable, satellites, PC terminals, browser interface, ISPs, routers and switches and modems and hubs. The next aspect to understanding the change potential of a network world is this: the network is not the infrastructure; it is a new venue for human interaction. A city is not really about its tall buildings, nor its long aqueducts, nor its grand Colosseum, but about its people, about how citizens get together. In just this way, the network will let us redefine how all of us get together. And this redefining will begin in earnest the moment people forget about the network as simply architecture.

The big change begins not when we reach a billion networked devices, nor when we get a billion people online. It begins in earnest when the network becomes normal, when it becomes indispensable, when it becomes as transparent as breathing.

This is already happening, through chat and e-mail and instant messaging. And cell phones.

The cell phone is a "normality precursor." As a phone, it is normal; we've been talking that way since the 1880s. It does what a phone does, but it does it everywhere: out in the open air, or in a car. And what phones do is to create an intimate space shared only by the two connected. You can be in a room full of people, or alone in the Himalayas, and suddenly you are in your own personal space with the person(s) on the other end(s) of the line.

These precursor network devices do not simply help the network become more "normal"; they make the network become needed, as in, "I can't live without it. My cell phone has become a part of me!"

People need to be connected to the ones they love. They need to be more effective with the ones they do business with. And so it is already coming to pass that most business happens in the network.

I don't mean to imply that all aspects of production will happen there—though a surprisingly large chunk of agriculture and industry will be network-driven. But the entire business of doing business, from transactions to collaboration to services and consultation, will be going on there. And as the network becomes a normal and natural

10